$2.75

We Tried to Stay

This is the story of an attempt that
seemed to fail. Young missionaries with fine
training, a sense of call, and a determination to succeed went to Hochwan in West
China to build a strong Christian center
there. They didn't go in order to turn around
and go home. They tried to stay. Yes, God
bless them, they did. They put their hands
to the plow with no thought of turning back.

But the Communist "liberation" swept the
country. American government authorities
warned them to leave. They were not afraid
to take the risk of staying. Their mission
board gave them permission to come home,
but left the decision to them. They decided not to go home. Local pressures became
unpleasant. They adapted their program,
but did not drop it. Then came the incident
which was made the excuse for Don's arrest
and deportation.

Dorothy, his wife (and the author of this
moving story), had to carry on until her
baby was born. Her clever courage, and
that of her missionary companions, will re-
store your confidence in the human race, at
least in the feminine part of it.

Even though they all finally got out of
China, they still wanted to stay. Love for
the land and the people oozes from the pores
of the book. The persecutors do not appear
as fiends, but as very lovable and very human creatures.

You can't read this book with a straight
face or with dry eyes. Here is one very intense episode in the history of the retreat of
Western missionaries from China. It is more
than clever writing; it is the pulse-beat of
Christian hearts.

PAUL ERB

We Tried to Stay

We Tried to Stay

Dorothy S. McCammon

HERALD PRESS . SCOTTDALE . PENNSYLVANIA

*To Esther and Enmei,
inseparable names in my treasury
of greathearted, God-given friends.*

Preface

This is not my book; it belongs to a multitude of people. It belongs to our many friends, both Chinese and foreign, who brought these experiences into being. It belongs to my five American colleagues who variously shared the experiences. It belongs to our church and our Mission Board who commissioned us to go to China. And it belongs to our daughter Julia; one reason it was written was so that she could read it fifteen years from now!

It belongs, too, to the many who have helped in its physical preparation. Our families carefully saved our letters and articles, and I have freely quoted from them. My patient husband was often the literal chief cook and bottle washer during the weeks of manuscript preparation. My sister typed many long hours, and kept Julia many more, and my mother proofread the final copy.

A number of friends gave time to reading the manuscript, and offered helpful advice and criticism. J. D. Graber, Secretary of our Mission Board, was kind enough to review the manuscript and write the introduction; Doris Davis Kurtz helped greatly by checking for weakness of continuity and the use of unfamiliar terms as she read; Esther Stockwell, who lived these same years and many more in China, represented those who tried to stay, as she read and gave good counsel.

The map was prepared by my husband Don, and credit for most of the pictures used should go to him. The balance of the pictures were taken by other members of our group, or by Rev. F. Olin Stockwell, a Methodist missionary.

To all of these I owe a real debt. Were this a flawless work which would do them credit, I would cheerfully say it was theirs. But there are plenty of imperfections, shortcomings, and inaccuracies which are purely my own. The reader will quickly recognize that this is my first attempt in the literary world.

Of this I am sure—that all who have had any part in the preparation of this work join me in the wish that the reader will not just be entertained. It is our hope and prayer that God may use this book to inform, inspire, and give renewed faith and courage to all who are concerned for His church in China.

DOROTHY S. McCAMMON

Middlebury, Indiana
November 4, 1952

Introduction

China has changed. It will never be the same again regardless of what might happen in war and politics. We have definitely come to the end of an era in China. This book is not a missionary report as such. The author has no viewpoint to defend or any system to condemn. Hers is simply a task of honest narration. But this does not mean that it is dull reading. Far from it, for many times we find proof of the adage that "truth is stranger than fiction," and this strange truth has been told in a most refreshing manner.

The descriptions and narrations of this book are not mere factual reporting. They breathe of love and devotion and of a warm Christian understanding. Five young American Christians answering a clear call of God to live and teach the Gospel of Christ in West China began their task with singular devotion and high idealism. We see hearts beating in unison and bands of love and friendship being forged right across racial and national lines. A family of Jesus is being formed; the kingdom of God is drawing nigh; and then comes tragedy! A ruthless negation by a new ideology of all they had lived and taught. More than that, all these delightful experiences are now being viciously interpreted and made to appear derogatory to China, an expression of a satanic western imperialism.

Although this interpretation of mission work is essentially false, it has yet a basis of validity. The dealings of the West with China during the centuries have been of an imperialistic nature. It is a fact that China was robbed of a great deal of her sovereignty. What seemed innocent or even for the good of China twenty-five or seventy-five years ago now looks quite different in the setting of a nation newly awakened to a radical national consciousness.

Inadvertently western missionaries adopted the so-called colonial viewpoint and did many things that can now be made to look exactly like a part of the imperialistic pattern. Events in China have shaken us rudely. We wake and find that a new day in foreign missions has dawned, and that we are living in a new world. Our attitudes, our policies, and our pattern of living in foreign countries are in for a drastic re-evaluation and change.

This process we see unfolding in *We Tried to Stay*. The experiences of this small missionary group in West China from 1947 to 1951 compress the history of a century, as it were, into a few swift years of change. When they first arrived in Hoch-wan they were completely in the "Old China" with its leisure-liness, quaintness, and its colonial outlook. When they left, the fierce furnace of the New Order was ruthlessly consuming the old and forging the new. One feels instinctively that many precious values of the past are being sacrificed and lost. Passions are much too hot and outside influences too potent for wise judgment. But the fire has been kindled; violent change is in process and what will eventually emerge will bear little resemblance to the "good old days." It will be a really new order.

In their decision to stay after "liberation" our missionary group best demonstrated their love for China and their faith in the new order. They knew the old order was changing and recognized that it needed changing. They believed they could go along with the change and that the opportunity for witness and evangelism would remain. In this they were mistaken, but they proved the sincerity of their call to China and their dedication to the missionary task they received from God.

This narration of the experiences of a group of missionaries passing through the furnace of "liberation" is not written because it is unique or even unusual. Such experiences have been tragically common among missionaries in all parts of China, sometimes with a much less happy outcome. These are published mainly because they are typical of the trials and frustrations through which many others were forced to go.

As we look back on these four years of triumph and defeat in West China we cannot escape the question, "Was it worth while?" This story of failure on the human level may well represent victory on a higher level. Who will say that our mission in China failed? No one will say that, but some might say that in view of what happened it was a waste of effort, time, and money.

No, it was not a waste. Judas called Mary's act of pouring out precious perfume in devotion to Jesus waste. Jesus disagreed. It is highly worth while when personal, spiritual, and material wealth is poured out in devotion to Christ. If He is pleased by the gift, and if He commends, then it has been eminently worth while.

Elkhart, Indiana

> J. D. GRABER, *Secretary*
> *Mennonite Board of Missions and Charities*

Contents

Illustrations

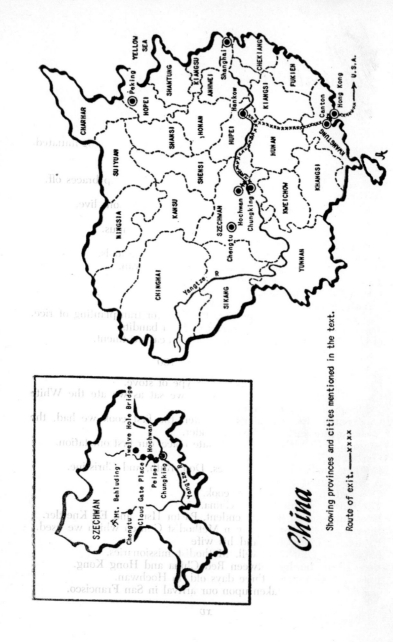

China

Showing provinces and cities mentioned in the text.

Route of exit.——xxxx

1. Retrospect

A year ago today I prayed to God that I would be arrested by the Communist officials in Red China. It seems almost fantastic as I write, surrounded as I have been this past year with the comforts of home, the security of our land, and the joys of family life. But it was real then! It was the last day of April, and May 1 was a big holiday for Communist China. All of the month of April soldiers and civilians were getting ready, with daily rehearsals for parades, laborious preparation of elaborate floats, lanterns and costumes, and carefully worded banners affirming undying love and loyalty to the People's Government in general, and Chairman Mao in particular. Not at all spontaneous to be sure, but very typical of the loyalty demonstrations required by the new regime.

Why, you ask, did I hope to spend such a gala day in prison? Not just because the primary slogan was "down with American imperialists," and the favorite marching song, "Kill Americans," but because my husband had been deported, my application for exit permit was being ignored, step by step my foreign colleagues' applications were being processed, our first baby was soon due to arrive, and it appeared as though the only chance I had to escape being left alone under difficult circumstances was to be sent out "in disgrace." Our neighborhood district and all local Christians had been ordered to hold meetings, at which time any grievance against any foreigner was to be aired. So it was that I truly was praying that someone would have a charge against me. Of course I wanted just the right degree of "crime"—important enough for immediate de-

·1·

portation, but not serious enough for detention! I had visions, yes and hopes, of being a leading figure in the May Day parades—exhibit A under the imperialistic American section. But that wasn't how the Lord had planned it. I write today to give testimony to the truth that God's grace is sufficient, His promises are sure, His ways are higher than our ways, and His wisdom is perfect. Nor was it just in times of stress that we found Him so. Come with me quickly through our short China term, and see for yourself.

We had ample opportunity to prove these truths in the years 1947-1951. From the day we arrived, we moved under the shadow of impending darkness in that great land. But we moved in peace to the last day, for we were also abiding under the shadow of the Almighty.

We had not been in China a week till we were convinced that we dared not visit our relief stations to the north—the risk of not returning was too great. At the time of our trip inland by river, there was considerable tension among our fellow passengers. Rumor said that fighting had come all the way south to the Yangtze in spots, and some passenger boats were actually being escorted by gunboats. Our year in language school was one long series of dark rumors and sobering realizations as refugee missionaries continued to arrive from the north.

We proceeded in the fall of 1948 to our own station, and during the first exhilarating week of unpacking and settling we received this message from our district Consular officials: "In view of the generally deteriorating situation, and the likelihood that means of exit from China may later be unavailable, all American citizens in Chungking Consular District who are not prepared to remain in areas where they now reside under possible hazardous conditions should plan *at once* to move to places of safety."

But we *were* prepared, and we did remain, nor have we ever had any regrets. We were only grateful that our Mission Board trusted our judgment enough to leave the decision to us. We saw daily and fearful demonstrations of the powers of darkness as the "liberating" armies came in, but we saw hourly and thrilling manfestations of the greater powers of Light. Share them now with us as we start at the beginning and relive some of the high lights of those epoch-making years.

2. We Enter China

"Please, thank you, Mrs. American, just a few thousand dollars for my poor mother, more than fifty years old," pleaded the sore-covered beggar on the Shanghai street corner. But I held tight to my roll of bills, recalling that my own mother was also more than fifty and she had no few thousand dollars. It was our first day in China, and the idea of a thousand being worth 2½ cents was not yet real to me!

We five had spent a pleasant month from New York to Shanghai, come unscathed through the customs inspection, and were out to get our first glimpse of the land we had long yearned to see. Five young missionaries, in a land new to our church, going to a station not even determined as yet, to live in a not-yet-built home on a not-yet-purchased lot, there to begin a to-be-decided-upon work: a nurse, Luella Gingerich; a dietitian, Christine Weaver; a teacher, Ruth Bean; and a minister and his wife, Don and I, from very different backgrounds but with a common goal. We were completely green at world traveling, but equally sure that God would guide us. Each of us had a peculiar sense of being called to China. In fact, every one of us had China in his heart before our Mission Board even announced the opening of that field. Such a sense of call was vital to our peace of mind in the tumultuous days which lay ahead of us, for ours had been sheltered lives and soon we were to see our hopes and dreams collapsing as the enemy came in like a flood.

My first Shanghai letter home records these impressions:

"How good it was to see Harriet Burkholder at the pier,

waving! Soon we were off the boat and meeting her and the other Mennonite Central Committee folk who had come to welcome us. The men got us through customs with our hand luggage, and the next day all our trunks and barrels went through without a cent of duty! A great deal of the deciding is left up to the particular customs official, and the one our group got was sympathetic with our mission program. Of course, all of us have freight coming later, and we aren't likely to be that fortunate again.

"Shanghai is positively the noisiest spot we've ever seen; everyone honks or bangs or yells instead of looking where he's going. But when we come in, we find a very peaceful and comfortable home. The MCC Hostel has very elastic accommodations, and this week we're stretching them pretty far—there have been seventeen at the table. A number of relief workers are in the city on business, and you can imagine the chatter which goes on from morning till night, with their news of each other and our news from the States.

"The biggest thing we have to get used to right away is the ridiculous money situation. Imagine at a Sunday-school committee meeting, hearing the teachers report that the primary department brought in $50,000 for a contribution toward their new chairs! There are three rates of exchange—official, open market, and black market. They vary from $12,000 to $1 to $85,000 to $1, and our heads fairly whirl when we try to do shopping, for we must compute what it would be in 'gold.' A lot of prices aren't too much different than ours at home; but the bill for our group's mail which we sent upon arrival was $285,000, and the check for a feast we enjoyed together one of our first days came to almost a million. Money is nothing to steal—people walk along with great gobs of it. Hundred-dollar bills are practically extinct; we get it in packs of a million at a time. The offering plate this morning in church resembled a bird cage, with a hole in the top to stuff in bills. Don put in $50,000.

"One of the first things we must get used to in China is that life just doesn't click along very fast; patience becomes not only a desirable virtue but a necessity. If there isn't a plane this week, maybe there'll be one next; and if no boat this month, surely they will have one before Christmas."

Don has the family eye for detail; so I will share some of his Shanghai letter to show you more of the city:

"Streets full of pedicabs, [rickshas powered by a man riding a bike instead of pulling], trucks, jeeps, small foreign cars, rickshas, two-wheeled carts with unbelievable loads, and milling people in throngs. Many streets can hardly be walked through in the mornings while everyone has food to sell. There are stands of fish heads, tails, or even entrails. By the bushel one can buy dried minnows (little but brown streaks any more) or live fish. Live ducks and chickens are kept in big woven baskets. Raw meat hangs out in the open—some old and drying, and some almost dripping. One stand has scraped pig tails—nothing more. Another man sells crabs by the string load. There one sells little bundles of sticks, another round lumps of coal dust squeezed together while wet. Women have great baskets of beautiful flowers—a dozen or two for a few cents, after one bargains a bit. One has a great basket of string beans; another Chinese celery; another a kettle of small, peeled potatoes. Some bake little things before one's eyes. Everywhere are great bunches of bananas, tangerines, things like grapefruit but whose sections are rather dry and sweet (pomelo, I think they are called), persimmons, and sections of sugar cane. Little sidewalk eating places serve an endless variety of snacks. Beef is hauled down the streets uncovered— not in American halves but cross cut. Men go along carrying goats' heads. Others pick up cigarette butts and reroll the tobacco with their rollers so they can resell it. I've watched the river junks unload coal—men carrying a heavy basket of the fine stuff between them on a bamboo pole. Women stand around to sweep up what trickles out as they walk along. That's their fuel supply—as well as for those who pick up small papers, or sweep up the crumbs of the manure cakes as they are hauled away. They constantly grunt and chant as they carry loads—unbelievably heavy loads on their necks and shoulders —up steps or narrow boards. Shops vary of course—some have very nice goods. They are nearly all open-front affairs, shut at night by foot-wide vertical panels. Most big buildings here seem to be banks. Money is carried in great boxes. There are no metal coins."

Days and weeks of postponements and change of plans. ("Go to now, ye that say, To day or to morrow we will go into such a city, and continue there a year, . . . whereas ye know not what shall be on the morrow!") Then the three girls were actually off for Chengtu, via Chungking by plane, and Don and I were on a Yangtze river boat with the freight, bound for Chungking.

I wrote: "We've seen, in the last day and a half, more of God's handiwork in natural splendor and beauty than either of us has seen in the first quarter century of our lives. The whole trip has been scenic and delightful, but two days ago we came suddenly into the Yangtze Gorges and for these hours since we have been sailing in a very narrow channel, up exciting rapids, and surrounded by three- and four-thousand-foot precipitous cliffs, done in exquisite colors. Now we are just as suddenly through the last gorge and our whole group is almost relieved and exhausted—so much beauty in so short a time is actually hard to absorb!

"The newspaper notice of the *Ming Ben's* arrival and departure at Shanghai said we would carry 220 passengers. Our conservative guess is that there must have been nearly a thousand. There were eight foreigners; all the rest Chinese. Five of us came across the Pacific together on the *Lynx*: Don and I, two men from the United Church of Canada, and a Methodist girl from Kansas. All three of them are veteran missionaries so have helped us immensely in knowing what to do next. The sixth is a Canadian lady who represents Canadian Aid to China in Shanghai. She took a second-class ticket not knowing that all her cabin mates would be Chinese men; so we have made room for her among us up in first-class. The seventh is a Britisher, who embodies all the typical British traits there are; he is a high official with the Salt Administration with a wealth of information and good stories. The eighth is a Catholic priest, whose only communication with us was to find out if any of the men were priests. I don't know where he keeps himself.

"We foreigners eat together, Chinese food, three times a day, with chopsticks. Don and I are amazed at how quickly we learned when getting the food depended on it. Don kids me a bit; says I would have turned up my nose at fried peanuts and rice for breakfast at home, but believe me, it tastes good here and I'm just glad it isn't shrimp complete to the whiskers, or century eggs, as we have had a few times. There are usually six dishes; so three or four are bound to be palatable."

We left Chungking as quickly as possible, for we were already late to language school, and when it is Chinese one is studying, a day is nearly as a thousand years we found! When we got a breathing spell, these impressions of a beginner took form:

"Chungking is a city of hills, and we started our experiences with them the minute we got off the boat. We had to climb several hundred steps to get to the truck that was waiting for us. A friend of ours had warned us not to take a chair ride up the steps. He said he never got a bit seasick all the way across the Pacific; never got a bit airsick all the way in to Hankow; never was as sick in his life as he was riding a chair up those Chungking steps! Chungking is of course still repairing its wartime damage. One of the missionaries there told us that in 1945 one could stand in the middle of the city and look a mile in any direction and see not one building standing. They have made a remarkably quick comeback, though much of the work is only of a temporary nature.

"We flew from Chungking to Chengtu in about an hour, coming over quite high mountains and rugged barren country, then suddenly finding ourselves on the contrasting Chengtu plains—flat, colorful land, divided into thousands of tiny patches, no two the same shape but all meticulously cultivated by hand. We thought at the time that perhaps distance hid the weeds and irregularities of planting, but close-up views of much farm country since has proved to us that the Chinese surely are the world's best farmers. Of course they need to be mighty efficient in their land utilization, and they have time to be, too. The results are beautiful.

"A warm welcome awaited us when we got to the University campus. Because we are planning eventually to go into a field that is now under Methodist supervision, the Methodists have been especially cordial. They had ideal arrangements all made for our housing. Ruth lives with Dr. and Mrs. H. S. Liljestrand, on the Methodist Compound. Christine and Luella are right next door with Rev. and Mrs. Olin Stockwell. We are just across the road on the Friends' Compound, living with an English Quaker, William Sewell. His wife and children are in England; so he had room to take us in. Although we live in separate homes, we are already feeling very much at home in the others' houses; everybody has afternoon tea, and one doesn't need an invitation! Already we find ourselves calling these good folk 'Dr. Harry,' 'Ethel,' 'Olin,' 'Esther,' and 'Bill,' and we are looking forward to knowing them better.

"And now we're deep into the study of West China Mandarin; let me tell you how we go about it. The Missionary Training Language School is really quite separate from West China Union University. The leading organizer of our school is a part-time University staff member, Dr. J. E. Moncrieff, of the American Baptist mission. He is highly respected by our teachers for his Chinese, and is well qualified to explain grammatical structures, etc., to us. However, all of our regular teaching is done by Chinese. Our day starts each morning

at 8:30 with an hour's new material from Mr. Pan, the person-
ification of Chinese scholars, who has been doing this same
work for thirty-one years. He knows plenty of English, but
you'd never guess it from his first period performance. He
sticks strictly to Chinese, starting with what we know and
introducing new words into old sentence 'frames.' First
thing we know we have guessed it, and next thing we know
we are using it in our speaking vocabularies! We guess
around the class till someone hits the English meaning and
that lucky person is rewarded by a toothy grin and the upturned thumb of approval.

"After we've gotten our new material, we break up into
groups of two to a drill teacher and spend most of the rest of
the day till 3:30 in oral drill. Hannah Cole, a lovely red-
haired soprano from Philadelphia, is my partner. We utterly
wear out the little we know, using it in limited conversations
and trying to make variations on it, but it works! We are
learning; no doubt about it. There is a good system of
phonetic writing for Chinese language, and we started out
by easily learning to use it. This makes it possible for us to
record material without knowing Chinese characters. (There
are a mere 40,000 of these.) It is widely used in China, even
to some extent in printed material such as Bibles; so we will
continue to benefit by having it. This week, though, we have
started on learning the radicals—214 root symbols which are
used in all characters—at least one of them in each, that is.
And we are starting on character recognition; a task that will
never be finished as long as we live. By the way, there are
about forty of us studying, in every possible stage of development. Students usually stay at least a calendar year and
sometimes longer before they proceed to their ultimate fields.
The old hands say you always think you'll take plenty of time
for study after you arrive there, but you never do. So we're
anxious to get a lot into our systems before we go.

"West China Union University, or Hwa Shi Ba Campus,

is very beautiful, with a typical collegiate air about it. The grass and some of the trees are green all winter. The gray stone buildings would be drab in themselves, but every single one of them is trimmed in vivid colors, with an anything *but* drab effect. The University is supported jointly by the American Methodists, the American Baptists, the United Church of Canada, the English Society of Friends, and the Church Missionary Society of England. Each of these groups contributes to the teaching and counseling personnel, and several of the groups have made this a concentration center for other mission work as well; the result is a foreign community of over 200 persons. Instead of feeling plunged into a different society, we find it almost difficult to make enough contacts with the Chinese. Foreigners in Chengtu could live quite comfortably without ever learning the language, but we have work to do with the language, and are very eager to use it more.

"How, with China news as it is these days, dare we plan for the summer and next year and next twenty years? The answer is that we only walk by faith. China is indeed in a critical economic and political situation. The Communists and Nationalists are too far apart to hope for any reconciliation or compromise on paper. The present government is too far sunk, I think, for any loans to put it back on its feet. And both of them are so far from right that neither of them seems to offer any hope at all to the thinking class of Chinese who might be able to bring order out of chaos. It really seems as though there is going to be a rock-bottom ending to the present sinking situation, and then a long pulling out, when the new government, which will be Communistic, will finally have to learn to co-operate with the rest of the world. We don't know enough even to venture our immature opinions, but that seems to be the sanest thinking of those who have grown up with the so-called republic.

"To the masses, the coming of Communists is by no means

the worst thing they can think of. An English Friend, who called here yesterday, said he is sure the folks in his little village hope they *will* come. And the current feeling here is that the majority of the college students would go along with them if they did. A certainty is that foreign personnel would have to leave the field for at least a time, so that is one major reason why we, of course, don't want to see North China fall. It would be the beginning of the end of the present China.

"Students are quite a different class in China than America. Here they are the only group who can afford to stick their necks out and say what they think. They have no families, no jobs, and a certain love of adventure coupled with a tremendous loyalty to their country and a desire to see it improved. They are forever 'demonstrating' in one way or another to get a point across. Recently several were injured when they marched on the governor's office demanding cheaper rice. He sent his soldiers out to use the wrong ends of their guns on the youngsters! It is very interesting to us to see how tolerant the rest of the Chinese society is of them. In a real sense the future of China is staked on a few among the present students who won't be utterly gobbled up in rotten politics and selfish schemes which aren't much different than the war-lord days of old.

"A few rambling thoughts, as I review a typical trip across the campus and back. They're installing a sidewalk at the hospital: mostly mud with a little cement in the top layer, rubbed smooth with a stone, and immediately stepped on by everybody . . . . Dozens of women and children cracking rock from dawn till dark on our compound, getting ready to build a road. The rock was brought in squeaking wheelbarrows by half-naked men who waded into the river for it. It smells like it . . . . The gateman's wife jumps to her feet every time we pass; she still grins at the thought of the New Year's feast we gave them, when *we* served *them;* you can be sure it's an old story at the teahouse by now . . . .

A dear little *mei-mei* (little sister) friend of mine carefully demonstrates to me that she knows how to wipe the baby's nose with a hankie; then waits my praise for the very unusual act . . . . A shoeshine friend of eight gives me a better shine for a penny than you ever had for forty cents at home . . . . The paper boy at the campus gate is still moaning what Ruth insists is 'It's me, O Lord,' but few people buy his wares, for the paper is plastered on the compound wall and they can read it for nothing . . . . The youngsters on the way to the University practice school wait till they pass us, then say very stiffly, in English, 'How are you?' and run away . . . . Bill, our host, comes home from a fine feast at the home of the leading pathologist in China, muttering about Chinese customs. Says he never saw his hostess till he left, when she appeared only long enough to insist that the delicious food was really very bad . . . . Picked some white camellias from a tree in the yard for the table. They would cost $10 a dozen where most of you live . . . . Saw an enterprising young man picking fleas off his *yi-fu* (that's a garment, not an animal) and eating them. Says philosophical Bill, 'Why not? They've been eating him!' . . . Visited for a while with a young friend Don has made who comes from another University here. He's brought a pal who hopes to come and 'play' with Don often! Their word for play covers a lot of territory, it seems . . . . We pass a little shrine with burning incense sticks placed in front of some ugly statue, and realize again that China's worst need is not in the realm of material goods."

And so we settled down to language study, the long hard grind which was prerequisite number one for the job ahead. Luella insisted and we agreed that if we were supposed to read up and down our eyes would have been installed vertically. Before we left the task we were tempted to agree with the Jesuit who said that Chinese was invented by the devil to prevent the Chinese from getting the Gospel, and we were in full agreement with the man who said, "to acquire the Chinese language is a work for men with bodies of brass, lungs of steel, heads of oak, eyes of eagles, hearts of apostles, memories of angels, and lives of Methuselah." To his list I would add, "and with much of the grace of God."

3. Excursions

Our language school was more than just a place to learn to talk—it was a place to learn about China. Consequently when some unusual ceremony was taking place in the community, we were given opportunity to attend and observe. I should like to tell you of three such excursions we made. The first I can report only partially firsthand. I blacked out in the midst of it and had to be taken home!

It was around Chinese New Year time, and the streets were simply thronging with people. Horrible beggars, last-minute shoppers, hobbling lines of bound-footed, bead-wearing little old ladies stumping along in a holy parade, incense-laden temple-goers in abundance, but most were just idle sightseers like ourselves.

The first mistake we made was to go at all, and our second mistake was to go together. Between thirty and forty of us set off by ricksha for an hour's ride to a Buddhist temple. There was a huge three-day celebration going on there, about like a fair, and within the temple grounds milled literally thousands and thousands of spectators. Unfortunately they were not by any means single-purposed pilgrims, and the arrival of a group of forty "high-nosed" (our bridges are higher) foreigners caused more of a sensation than the holy rites proceeding all about them. Our teachers had arranged for us to attend, in a body, one service at which a group of young candidates were actually initiated as acolytes, or assistants to the priests. But the mob decided that wherever we went they were going too, and they closed in. It was fortunate that we had some husky men with us, for otherwise we women would surely have been crushed. The boys lined up in two solid lines and rushed us through the safety lane. We were ashamed at how rough they had to be just to get us safely where we were going. We were halfway there, and there was nothing to do but finish the trip, but it was a revolting demonstration of me-first-ness on our part. We were finally in the small room and the door was shut, but the angered mob thundered so loudly outside that I really expected them to crush in the flimsy side of the building. Eventually the clamor died down and the ceremony began.

The lads to be initiated looked sixteen to eighteen years old. They were led into the semidarkened room where they knelt on bamboo mats. Their hands were clasped and their faces and eyes upturned as in prayer. Nine spots had been marked on their clean-shaven heads, and now nine cones of incense were set on the spots and lighted. As they burned down, they burned into the scalp and killed the roots of the hair, thus marking the head for life. Of course it was an extremely painful process, but the boys were to utter no sound, only to pray silently as the cones glowed and finally died out.

The push of the crowd, the closeness of the room, the smell of the incense, the pained, sweat-streaked faces so close to my own—in combination it was too much. The next thing I knew someone was trying in vain to push my head between my feet. In vain, I say, because that day I had girded up a bit extra against the cold, and whalebone is tough! Christine and our cook's wife had also had enough; they braved the crowd with me and after a lesser version of the original crush, we got to rickshas and went home.

We heard the rest of the story later, how the boys kept perfect silence until the ashes were cooled, then were given tangerine sections to cool their lips and were quietly walked up and down in the adjoining courtyard until they had regained their composure. I never met a dotted head again without recalling that exciting day, and feeling a touch of nausea.

Later on we language school students took a day off from our studies to make a bus journey to Kwanhsien, a small city some twenty miles north of Chengtu. There were many interesting side lights, but the main item of interest was the opening of the dam. I wrote this when I got home that day:

"This day of the opening of the floodgates is of great significance in the lives of the people of the Chengtu Plain, because it assures them of a good crop during the summer months. Kwanhsien is the head of the irrigation system which provides a water supply for about two thirds of the plain, or about 1,000 square miles. The dry creek beds which we passed as we drove toward Kwanhsien were soon to be filled, and from them will flow smaller man-made channels, until finally each farmer's beautifully built-up rows will be surrounded by as much water as he wants them to have; then he will merely stop up the opening in his handmade dike and the water will flow on again. Little wonder it is a real holiday for the farm folk.

"There were thousands there before we arrived, attending ceremonies and offering sacrifices of pigs and lambs at two temples. The first temple was built because of fear. It was erected to a child who turned into a dragon, and whose thrashings about were supposed to have been the cause of the many floods in centuries gone by. The second temple was erected in gratitude to a king who devised the present system of digging channels throughout the plain, and holding back the water by dams until it is needed. This wise king was so thorough in his planning that to this day his ideas are followed. He had buried at the head of the channel two huge iron bars. Each spring when the channel is cleaned out, prior to the opening of the waters, the laborers know when they reach those bars that they are far enough.

"After satisfactorily appeasing their heathen idols, the masses proceeded to the actual ceremony of the opening of the dam. Early in the day, the supports of the dam had been sawed in several places, to weaken the structure. At a given signal, a long line of coolies pulled on a huge rope, and the first support broke away, letting a trickle of water come through. A great shout rose from the crowd, some of whom *kow-towed* (bowed the head) as the water approached, and many of whom were eager to throw a stone into the stream, thus assuring themselves of a successful and prosperous year.

"Such outings are pleasant, of course, but always we find ourselves returning home impressed primarily with the pitiful futility of such beliefs. And again and again we come home overwhelmed with the terrible urgency and wonderful adequacy of the Gospel we have been called to proclaim— the Gospel of the saving grace of Jesus Christ.

"Since this trip I've found myself thinking happily of the not-too-distant time when we can speak more clearly to these same people about the most important thing in their lives. I think one of the stories I want to tell them will go something like this:

"'Without Christ, dear friends, your lives are just as those river beds were before that king devised an irrigation system. Sometimes they are dry and arid, and sometimes wild and tumultuous, but always uncontrolled, without guidance, and without purpose. There is much near at hand which your own lives could touch and help, but not without first making some major changes in them.

"'The love of God is like that Tung River up beyond Kwanhsien; only waiting to be found and appropriated. It has always been there, and is meant for you, but you have not always known. It can bring life and joy and happiness to you now, just as the Tung River fills a need in your daily lives. But much more than that—much, much more—it can bring life eternal to your souls.

"'Jesus Christ is our Way—our *yen*—our dam—through which this love of God can enter our lives. He is the only way the Lord has provided for this water—this Water of Life— to enter your dry and thirsty hearts.

"'And what must you do? What is your part? Only this: To open the gates as those coolies do each year. Your part is to pull on that rope from within your own hearts, and to let this life-giving water, this love of God, enter through the only *yen*—the only Way—Christ.'"

❋   ❋   ❋

You may weary at my references to the importance of "having a friend," but truly in China that was the skeleton key which unlocked any door. One lovely occasion I shall never forget came about like this:

The principal of the Methodist Girls' High School had taught the various daughters from a wealthy Chinese home for years. Often they invited her to their home. This year they were so thoughtful as to suggest she bring some friends along and I was fortunate to be one of those chosen.

We were invited to see their chrysanthemum gardens, but as the weather was unpleasant, they brought the flowers into the house. What a room! Perfectly appointed according to Chinese tastes, and simply full of beautiful 'mums of every possible description. They brought only one of a kind. They said they have more than 10,000 kinds, and I believe it. They showed display after display, artistically arranged in perfect vases, standing on specially built cases. That was more than enough beauty for one day, but only a beginning.

The next stage was to bring in white silk books, in which they had painted the prize flowers from each year's garden. The whole family is extremely artistic, and the four girls had taken turns at painting. They sketch the flower's general form and special points, put just a touch of color so that they'll remember, and then later spend a month or two painting it to perfection. They choose their own names, which are imaginatively descriptive. The books were really fine art and worth a small fortune, I'd venture.

Nor was that enough. The flower-loving brother had shown his special pride and joy, the painting sisters had shown theirs; next came the deaf-mute brother who did exquisite woodworking, polishing the pieces for months with special strokes of his hands, all in certain directions, only with oil and never with sweat. That was an art in itself. But the real high spot came when the elder brother took us—how funny it seems to us foreigners—through the kitchen and coal house and woodhouse and all the other unlovely spots to another beautiful tearoom, where we gasped over a thirty years' accumulation of museum pieces such as I never expect to see again. They chose about thirty out of their 200 pieces. Each one was in a specially built wooden case, satin lined, with the shape of the vase or dish or cup cut out of it, so that they fit in perfectly. The inner cover was of glass, and then a carved wooden front slid over that. After a tour through their garden, complete with pools and a small mountain for stargazing, we started eating dinner about four in the afternoon. We were invited for one o'clock! One of the guests counted forty-one dishes at the feast, but that included eleven combined in the climaxing *piece de resistance,* which featured—you guessed it—chrysanthemums! All dishes were served in pewter bowls with an alcohol fire under them.

You can well know that such homes were first targets when the Communists came. I heard before I left China that one of the brothers was in prison, another pulling a public ricksha for a livelihood, and the old family home with its treasures was of course completely taken from them. A pathetic touch was the story of one brother disguising himself as an old gardener, and slipping into his own gardens to salvage a few of his most precious roots.

4. We View the Land

Hochwan, "the coming together of rivers," was to be our home in China, and once it was decided upon, we could hardly wait to view the field. Don and Lawrence Burkholder made the final recommendations to our Board after a visit to the city in February, 1948, while we were in language school. Lawrence was stationed in Shanghai with the MCC, and was asked by the Board to counsel with us in this major decision. He flew out, and with Don and the Methodist representatives who had the oversight of this section, made a tour of the whole area. They came back full of enthusiasm, feeling that we girls should soon make the trip too. The people had been eager for our coming, and only regretted that we needed to wait till fall. A visit from us in the spring would assure them of our continued interest in them, and so in April we made our first pilgrimage. Here is part of my letter describing that journey:

"We left Chengtu April 22. They told us to be at the air office at 10:30 A.M.; so we left home about 9:45. At 4:00 P.M. we left the office for the field, and at 5:00 P.M. we flew for Chungking. A seven-hour wait sounds long, but we are gradually getting into the swing of China and just felt thankful that we flew the same day we were scheduled. Soon after our arrival in China someone told us about the epitaph which read, 'Here lies the foreigner who tried to hurry the Orient.' He died early, they said. We got to Chungking in a little over an hour. The air doesn't bother any of us. We rushed around getting boat tickets, return passage, and lunch lined up, and then to bed. The next morning at 4:00 A.M. we went to the boat office, and sailed about 5:30 A.M. up the Kia Ling River, which we pronounce *Jya Ling*.

"There is a daily motor launch up to Hochwan and one back to Chungking. It is 180 *li*, or about sixty miles. Our trip up took 11½ hours; back, five hours. The fare up is considerably more than the fare back, by the way. It is a scenic trip, but the day seemed awfully long. For one thing, we got very hungry, since we ate our lunch in the middle of the morning. But we were sitting where we could see the food prepared, and none of us were hungry enough to eat it. A couple of boys prepared it, cooking it in river water, tasting it with their fingers, serving it in bowls which were washed in cold river water and rubbed out with a black greasy cloth. After the bowls were washed they were set on the floor again where they all walked with their bare feet (not the bowls), then stacked into each other again. Any food that was left over from one sitting was dumped back into the pot, even though six or eight people had put their chopsticks into the common bowl and then into their mouths. The chopsticks were cleaned by all being held together in the fellow's hand, slopped around in lukewarm water a little, and the outside ones wiped off with the dirty rag. Incidentally, after dinner, the dishwashing pail was used by the entire kitchen crew to have foot baths; then they proceeded to prepare the next meal. Perhaps you will agree that we weren't that hungry!" (That was another first impression which changed. Later on we learned simply to sit where we couldn't see the kitchen, and nothing ever tasted any better than a hot bowl of fried rice and egg on a cold day! A lot depends on the point of view.)

Our first view of Hochwan was far from inspiring, and a closer view of the river-front area was still more depressing. On the river's edge were hundreds of wooden river boats, with only a few bamboo mats for a roof. These were homes for countless families. Here they were born, and here many died. A tiny stove in one end was the kitchen, the floor was the bed, the back seat was the sewing room, and the roof was the hen house. Tiny children sometimes had a stick tied to them to make it easier to fish them out when they fell overboard, but it was a rare boat trip to Chungking on which we didn't see at least one floating body. The boats were their livelihood as well as their home. Whenever there was something or someone to haul somewhere, away they went. If not, they parked in the sun, waiting and hoping for work.

On the shore as far as eye could see were hundreds of matchbox-like shacks. One spark gone astray could have wiped the bank clean. Something else did just that, always once and sometimes twice a year, we learned. That's why those poor folk lived there; nobody needed to pay rent on this floodland. Steps up to the city from the river numbered more than a hundred, but at flood time in the fall there were sometimes not a dozen steps out of the water. When the occupants of the shacks knew the flood was coming, they took down the tile laid on for a roof and stacked it neatly. They lashed the bamboo poles which had supported their house into a raft, tied it fast, laid the tile, the mats which were house siding, and their other valuables on the raft, and rode up with the flood. For weeks at that time of the year there were hundreds of local displaced persons. They would huddle along the city wall, using the wall for one side of a temporary shelter. A bamboo mat propped against the wall completed their triangular home. Grandmas, babies, pigs, chickens—the whole family existed in this house until the river receded. But to get back to our arrival—

"We were met on the dock by a welcoming delegation, and whisked off to a round of entertainment. Friday night, Saturday, and Sunday, we were feasted until we should all have been sick. I guess the Lord knew we just had to eat that much, and kept us from perishing. We like Chinese food very much, but when people invited us even to break-fast, making three meals a day of peppery Szechwan fare, it was pretty hard. Various groups were host to us; the pastor, the whole church, the official board, the woman's society, and a couple of private individuals. An interesting example of 'face' and its importance: A lady who is church treasurer invited us for Monday; we needed to be gone to the out-station then. We explained it to her, but to no avail. Then we told the Chinese District Superintendent who also was there, and he fixed it up. The day the official board enter-tained us, we all knew it was at their expense, but to save her face they told the treasurer she could be hostess; so we made our bows and compliments to her, and she did all the proper remarks about how poor the food was. We never get used to that in China—all through the meal we must keep remarking about how good and how much it is, and if we slow down, they start remarking about the lack of variety and poorness of preparation. That is our cue to start gushing again!"

There was much we didn't comprehend then, to be sure, but we sized up the spiritual condition accurately, I see by another letter written home after that visit:

"We attended a business meeting of the congregation, there expressing our plans to come, about November 1, to stay. They all wished it could be sooner, and so did we, but we think Chengtu the best place to study. We've got to be able to comprehend quite a bit when we land in Hochwan, for there are going to be complications galore. All the churches of the chain we are taking on are in an appalling spiritual condition. Everyone involved admits it freely. Far too much of their warm welcome is based on the physical improve-ments they are expecting us to make. There are worse things than going into raw, unenlightened heathendom, and I think one of those things is going where people think they are all set spiritually when they are not. It will be most difficult.

Their leadership has been untrained, and as some of the Methodists told us, we will probably have to 'preach out' those who don't belong, and start over. We were particularly surprised by the idea one speaker presented, and which the others echoed from there on—that we were coming with a fourfold program: education, medicine, agricultural improvement, and evangelism. They usually had to think a bit to recall the last point. Their interest was too clearly in what they would receive in tangible goods. This is nothing peculiar to China; unregenerate man is the same the world around.

"North of Hochwan there are four outstations in a row. At none of them is there a pastor, and only at one is there anything left of the church. We four girls went along with the men on a tour of the stations, in spite of the horror of the only other foreigners in Hochwan, two German ladies affiliated with the China Inland Mission. These ladies objected so strongly that we asked the Methodist pastor to find a Chinese lady to go along—we would pay her way; but he said it was completely unnecessary. People knew we were Christians, and knew what our standards were, and he also added that the ladies were a bit behind the times! So off we went. We looked a fright—the ladies insisted on putting some of their age-old sun hats on us. We went seventy li up and really got into the backwoods. People were obviously scared of us; there were none of the friendly 'mis-i-ter, *ding how* [very good]' greetings that we got in Chengtu and Chungking. Plenty of them had never seen foreigners before. It reminded me of the Bible's description of what the last days will be like—people just froze in their positions. I was particularly struck by one little street we went through. A barber shaving a child's head with one more lock of hair, stopped in his tracks with his razor in the air. A little farther on, a mother stood holding a vomiting child; another lady tried to attract her attention to it, but the lady just stood looking at us, with the baby throwing up all over her.

"A stop at one outstation was pathetically awful. Ed Knettler, the District Missionary, had been there two months before, and there was absolutely no life to be found in the church. He had encouraged Pastor Hsu from Hochwan to try to stir up something. When we went in, there sat a whole table of men gathered, and what did the District Superintendent do but conduct quarterly conference! Ed about fainted. Neither the D.S. nor Pastor Hsu knew any of their names, but they called them the official board and the men looked very solemn and talked about the affairs of the church just as though there were a church. One man came in just when they were signing their names to the minutes of the meeting, and the D.S. said, 'Aren't you on the church board?' The man said no. The D.S. said, 'You've lived here for years, haven't you?' The man said yes. So the D.S. said, 'Sign your name; you're on the board.' His idea of church membership qualifications seems to be that the men don't smoke opium and the women aren't prostitutes. Understand me, this wasn't typical, but it was the pathetic efforts of some tired old men to please the young missionary.

"We went on to Shr Er Dung Chiaw (12-Hole-Bridge), and found a really challenging situation. About thirty Christians have held on, though they've had no local pastor for years. They get together every Sunday, read the Bible, review Bible stories, and pray for a pastor. They are the community leaders, including the principal of the kindergarten, the principal of the government middle school, the two village magistrates, and others. It is a very hopeful place on our list. They were most warm in their welcome.

"We recalled missionary stories when they showed us our beds for the night—tables of various heights pushed together; delightfully uncomfortable. I further followed tradition by entertaining fleas all night. I still can't get used to some of the lesser things, such as waking up and hearing a rat about two inches from my head. The next night I asked Don to look around with the flashlight before we turned in, just for my peace of mind, and he turned up a spider at least five inches across!

"Another thing I can't get used to is the different standards of modesty for women. We had communion at Hochwan, and when I returned from the altar I saw at least four women sitting with their breasts exposed. The children run around the church noisily, and stop in for refreshments when they get tired out. One of my neighbors at the altar fed her communion bread to her youngster. In the country farther north, I actually believe that more than 50 per cent of the women we saw had at least one breast uncovered, going about their various tasks. Christine thought maybe they were feeding on schedule now, and that we happened by at feeding time!

"Incidently, I made my classic 'first' which all missionaries seem to relate. Both nights in Hochwan, we conducted evangelistic services—I say we; it was mostly Ed, but we did help sing. The second night Ed asked me if I would like to teach a simple song; so I did. I explained it, said it, and they repeated after me, till we were ready to sing it. They learned it easily and well, and I was very happy till the next day the girls told me that when I concluded I had said, 'This song is very important, with a good meaning, easy to remember and easy to teach to others; so by all means *don't* remember it.' My face is still red!"

A very happy prospect for us was the friendship and companionship of the two German ladies living in Hochwan. Miss Barbara Janke and the Countess of Luttichau had been there for ten and thirteen years without furlough. They were naturally living somewhat in the past and we shocked them a bit, but we had confidence that we could learn to understand and appreciate each other. They owned the large foreign property which had once belonged to the Methodists, and welcomed us to live with them until we could build something. Their understanding of the Chinese, their disciplined lives, their love of the Lord—all of these would strengthen us as we lived near them. And it helped the Chinese Christians to learn something of unity in Christ; there was a decidedly unhealthy feeling between the two local church groups at first.

We came back from our visit sobered but challenged. In this valley were perhaps a million souls who knew little or nothing of Jesus Christ. "How then shall they call on him in whom they have not believed? and how shall they believe in him of whom they have not heard? and how shall they hear without a preacher?"

"O God, we are weak and unworthy, but Thou art able to make Thy strength perfect in weakness. Here are we; send us!"

5. White Deer Summit

It is an acknowledged fact that the *most* one can do in a Szechwan Province summer on the plain is to vegetate and endure. Since we were interested in accomplishing considerably more than that during our first summer, we took the advice of old hands and planned to study in the mountains. The language school and most of the foreign community divided itself between two mountain resorts. While some went to famous Mt. Omei, our plans worked out for Mt. Behludin (white deer summit) to the north of Chengtu. Our teachers went with us and we continued on much the same schedule as before. My first letter from the *din*, or summit, records some details of the trip.

"We packed and bought and did all kinds of things last week, hoping to leave on Monday. It rained all week, and we had a hard time keeping our courage up, because the roads go to squash in just a little while. On Sunday night Olin came home from an extended trip, and said we should not even consider leaving the next morning, but Don and George Cole, the two men of our party, were determined. Because Olin's doubts were based on the bridges' probably being out, he predicted that we'd spend several days somewhere along the way. But we planned to leave at 7:00 A.M. At about 8:00, the Coles and their two youngsters came, but their being late didn't matter because the truck was too full and we were throwing things off. We had bargained to haul more than we were capable of. And then the truck wouldn't start! The boys all cranked the big old thing until they were sick. Then they got some neighborhood servants to help and they pushed it up and down the muddy lane. They slipped and sloshed around till they looked as though they'd been on the trip already, but it didn't start. Finally Olin got out his jeep, or rather the boys rolled it out and pushed *it* until it started. They hitched the jeep to the truck, and finally the truck started. We dashed off and caught up with the truck, and tried to load into it. But we were seventeen people, and there was room for about six. So—with a couple of men on the fenders, one or two on the running boards, one sitting on the cab, etc., we were off. The day was terrifically hot, and the sun dried up a lot of the water. We progressed pretty well, though very slowly, for a good part of the way—then the bridges began. Don had located planks for the truck to carry, and on two bridges he and George put the planks across, we all unloaded, the driver prayed, and they guided him across. On both bridges the back wheels started to crumble the edges of the bridge and he gunned it over just in time. The bridges are so old and so narrow; they were built ages ago without a thought of a vehicle, of course.

"Then we came to the first long covered bridge. We started through all right, but the cover was so constructed that it got lower and lower. We crept along and soon things started cracking and the load started shifting—this with us women and children in the back of the truck. One by one the top covering braces of the truck cracked off under the canvas. We stopped and got off, and the men had to back the truck up, take off the canvas, lift off the broken braces, and rearrange the whole load. From then on we rode on top of the boxes and cases, watching for branches and wires and roofs that hung out too far. Often as we drove through narrow village streets we knocked down people's front porches—straw mat affairs that we just couldn't miss. Luella and I were clear on top in a most exposed spot, and got badly sunburned. Don and George kept encouraging the poor Scandinavian Alliance Mission drivers;

they wanted time after time to turn back, but Don and George would walk ahead and say it got better, and we would go on again. The last stretch was terrifically deep mud, practically no road; and when we slid in the mud we came awfully close to the edges and drop-offs. We were held up quite often by *ban ban che's*, push carts loaded with coal. There just wasn't room for a truck and anything else. One stream didn't have a bridge; so we drove through.

"If Olin's predictions of high water had been correct, we would have been in the same class with our Baptist friends who last year spent nine days on the trip, but the water was still in its banks and we got into Hiodza, the end of the line, that afternoon. We had hoped, and it was conceivable, to make the whole trip up to the bungalow in a day, but we got started too late and lost time on old bridges; so we didn't try. The Canadian mission has a Chinese pastor at Hiodza, and he was very kind. The boys put the baggage in the church and we spent the night there. Besides George, Hannah, Georgie, and Bethie Cole, we had our own five, our servants, and theirs, a 71-year-old retired Methodist pastor who is one of our teachers, Aunt Tee, a visitor from America who with her missionary niece, Alice Weed, will live with us this summer, and a dental student who is acting as business manager of the mountain association. We really looked just like a dust bowl local when we pulled in. We were dry as bones, burned to a crisp, dirty as we could be, and branches had ripped my clothes till I wasn't fit to be seen at all. The boys put up cots all over the place; we went out and ate some simple food, and turned in early. Before we did, though, we shocked the natives by all filing down to a deliciously cold stream and soaking our feet for a while. The church front is right on the street, and the whole town knew the church was full of foreigners; so about half the night was spent in listening to them bang on the boards, yell for foreigners, and set off firecrackers. Finally the noise died down, and it was quickly time to get up. We had some instant coffee and got the inevitable *kai shwey,* or boiling water. That with some leftover picnic from the day before got us going. Then began the brawl proper.

"Fortunately the local pastor did the bargaining with the carriers. When the doors were opened, the carriers swarmed in and practically tore the place down, each trying to find the lightest load. But when it was ended, they were paid by weight anyway; so it didn't matter. There were young men and old men, strong and crippled, women, little boys, and even girls, all with their carrying equipment of a rough jacket woven of leaves, and a big stick which doubled as a cane while walking and seat while resting. They looked like tripods every time they stopped to rest. Eventually all our goods started off, being carried on the backs of the carriers—eighty-eight pounds to a person, for the most part. We found enough *huagans* to carry the people who needed it most, and sent them along too. *Huagans* are reclining seats carried by two people. Don went along on foot, to watch our things, or at least to give the impression that they were being watched. Coles and I stayed behind to see that everything got taken, and that the cook remembered to buy what we needed. When we were ready to start, there wasn't another *huagan* in town; so we walked.

"The first several miles weren't bad, although there wasn't any shade anywhere. But then we started up. The only water we had was boiling hot—the only kind it's safe to buy, and we hadn't had opportunity to cool it. So you can imagine what a comfort it was when we were melting. We had to cool it cup by cup in streams before it was fit to drink. We had one quart for six adults and Georgie. Things went from bad to worse as we all got more tired—none of us were in physical condition for such an undertaking. We had to stop and get our wind every few minutes, and it was immediately gone again it seemed. The servants were getting green as grass, and George was just pulling Georgie. Hannah and I were going faster, then resting oftener than the others. About the time we thought we were going to lie down on the path and die, we began to overtake our carriers who had started several hours earlier. Finally we came to one who had canned goods! We pounced on the goods; George ripped off the slats with his bare hands. The first can was relish, then baking powder, and next corned beef, but in the bottom we found a gold mine—three cans of tomatoes. George tore the can open with his knife and we ate with gusto. The servants who detest tomatoes, reached right in the can and ate with their bare hands, too. At least tomatoes were cold and wet.

"The going got steeper and steeper, and just when we were about to another stalemate, we met a youngster coming down with his hoe from a cornfield. George asked him how much he'd charge to carry four-year-old Georgie to the top. He grinned all over his face, said 'you name the price,' grabbed Georgie on his back, and disappeared over the next hill. The Lord sent that lad, no fooling. Soon after that we came to a marvelous stream, as clear and cold as our wildest imagination could have dreamed up. We saw that Georgie was safely out of sight, and then dipped in. We drank till we hurt. When we were full we looked up the hill and saw the usual cornfield, but all I can say is that anybody who would carry night soil (human excrement used for fertilizer) up that steep hill isn't typical. And in closing may I add that if this is my last letter and I die of typhoid tomorrow, that was the best drink of water I've ever had in my life.

"About that time it started to rain, and we were like cold rats from then on. We thought we were almost there until we came around the last corner, and there stuck Behludin, straight up another 800 feet or so, and I do mean straight. They call the last stretch 'The Devil's Staircase' and a good name it is. George says he could fend off the whole Communist army with a pea shooter from there; just sit at the top and blow on them. I say if they're enterprising enough to come up after us I'll go

4

along quietly. This is probably the safest place in all of China. Hannah and I couldn't look up—we just took about five steps and sat down in the mud, then another five. By this time it was slippery as anything, the soil being clay, and the rain ruining any foothold. In spite of my lack of energy, I could still laugh at Hannah, usually a real diplomat with her children. Georgie was whining, wanting to get down and walk. She finally said, without a glint of humor in it, 'Georgie Cole, if you don't shut up I'm going to hit you over the head with this umbrella,' and his father added coldly, 'and then we'll roll you down the mountain.'

"We arrived in a pouring rain at the Coles' cabin. Hannah put on her cook's wife's dress and I wore a big coat till Don got word we were here and brought down some dry clothes. We sat around and ate creamed salmon with each other's spoons till the carriers all arrived. When we paid them off, I guess we paid at least thirty carriers plus the *huagan* carriers with a total of $7 gold. And they were satisfied it was a good bargain. We were too!

"Once here, this place is simply marvelous. We are only 6,000-7,000 feet high, but it makes a lot of difference. We can look across and see the river valley, the Chengtu Plain, the Snow Mountains on the other side, in fact, mountains in all directions. Sometimes the clouds are below us, sometimes rolling in our windows; sometimes the sun is shining across the way. Just now we're hoping for rain to fill our huge casks so that we don't need to carry water from a lower cabin. We're next to top house in the community. The first job the men did was to fix up our giant rain-water catcher and put wooden eaves on the house. They've also made us buckets, and completely rebuilt the stove in the kitchen."

We were continually entertaining the mountain folk, who took the day off to peer at us much as we might go to the country fair. Often they asked for clothing, or had something to sell, and one family even offered us their children!

Ours was a poverty-stricken valley below. One day after a marketing expedition our cook showed us a dry cake the natives were eating, made partly from dirt. The Good Earth is not just a book. So it was that we could not be too surprised when bandits came to our community.

It was after a violently stormy Saturday night, and we were all inspecting the damage lightning had done to our house. A tree in front was hit and the bolt entered our house, breaking windows, throwing a piece of the wall across the room, cracking and riddling a plaster wall just beside Aunt Tee, who slept safely on a rubber mattress, and even numbing our feet as we lay in bed! When our neighbor, Mrs. Phelps, toiled up the hill, we all rushed out to show her and tell her. When we finally finished, she told us a story that made ours sound mild!

The armed bandits had struck during the worst of the storm, starting at the home of our language school principal, Dr. Moncrieff. He heard his wife scream, and going to her assistance found her being beaten by the bandits. Then they turned on him and beat him severely too. After that they took rings, glasses, money, watches, flashlights—anything they could get their hands on. They forced the young Chinese student who was managing the camp to accompany them from house to house. They called at several other cabins, making off with a lot of valuables. Finally, before they got as high as our house, the young manager convinced them that morning would soon be upon them and they had better flee; so we were spared. Next morning at our church service Dr. Moncrieff and other victims expressed their gratitude to God that it had not been worse. Two of the men went to the foot of the mountain to report the episode, but the heavy rain had swollen the stream out of its banks and they could only tie a note to a rock and throw it across.

We foreigners almost came to regret reporting it at all, for the local version of justice was pretty awful. They brought some suspects up and tortured them, hanging one by his thumbs until they came off, and eventually shooting one, we heard.

Soon after that the neighboring valley started echoing with gun shots, and we were amazed to learn that a remnant of the Boxer days still carried on near by. A group of bandits called the Red Lantern Society terrorized the country people, claiming that bullets would not penetrate them. We were told this by people who really believed it themselves.

This combination of terrors plus the usual threats from the north brought a flock of the local militia to guard us, and they spent the rest of the summer living on the back porches round about. Of course they freely admitted that if any trouble came, they wouldn't stay to see what happened! And we privately surmised that if their ancient firearms were loaded at all, they likely had to hold a match to them to set them off.

The end of August brought us back down the mountain before the streams were uncrossable. Our hill friends looked amazed at the speed with which these long-limbed individuals came swinging and singing along, and when I got home I gathered that maybe we did come a little too fast. Both big toenails were completely black for weeks from banging into the ends of my shoes!

At the foot of the mountain we found summer in full swing, after two luxurious months of wearing woolens and sitting by the fireplace. After a day of walking and one of ricksha bumps, we were mighty glad to see Olin waiting in his jeep. He just came out on a hunch, he said, thinking we might come and knowing we would be weary. When we got to Chengtu, our three homes had a picnic supper waiting, complete with ice cream and lemonade. You're right. There are a lot of good people in the world.

6. Settling In

When we came to Hochwan to live in the fall of 1948, we quickly felt at home. The German ladies made ample room for us in their big house, and we girls went on with language study while Don built the house. His work was surely language study too, but not of a type that helped him much in his vocation. I dare say some of the everyday terms he picked up from the workmen would have created quite a sensation from the pulpit! We attended all the services connected with the church, gradually learning to know the people and to understand some of their language.

Here are details which Don wrote home, soon after we arrived:

"Service theoretically starts at ten o'clock, but since few people have reliable clocks, it's not the custom to be any place at the time named. Ten-twenty is more likely the starting time. So it was today. Arriving at ten o'clock, we found tall, old, white-bearded Pastor Hsu visiting with several men while waiting for people to come. The church building has a typical interior: the floor of cut stone, rather crude wooden benches, and a low, simple pulpit; the front wall is white with large characters in black occupying the center portion—God's Ten Commandments are always before the people; on the right is the Lord's Prayer and on the left, the Apostles' Creed; high in the center is a large single character which means 'love.'

"Soon the pastor rang a little school bell, told three boys in front to sit down, and the service began with prayer. The first song was announced and the organist began to play. They have no song leader; so many began singing late. Several times the organist had to stop to see whether everyone was singing.

"After reading the Scripture, Pastor Hsu began to preach. A departure from our method is the use of a large blackboard where he had written twelve special points of his sermon. After expounding one point, he would turn and read the next one to be emphasized. Lest that sound rather long, I should mention that an alarm clock was on the pulpit to guard the time. During the sermon, a large dog wandered up and went to sleep by the pulpit. No one paid any particular attention to it; so I assumed that this was a common incident. Distractions, unfortunately, were many. Children are not in any way trained to be quiet, and grown people talk to their neighbors with unlowered voices. It seemed that one might well teach greater reverence in the Lord's house—but we must not condemn such things too quickly, for the Chinese do not have a society where quietness is the desired or expected thing. Nonetheless, proper teaching would, I'm sure, make the value of quiet reverence understood and appreciated. It is one of many tasks before us.

"After the sermon, the pastor took some bills from his pocket and placed them in the collection basket, inviting the congregation to do likewise. Thereupon people singly and in groups went forward, left their offerings, and returned. After the giving of thanks and the singing of two verses of song, the service was ended."

It became apparent that very few of the group which had originally welcomed us to Hochwan were really a part of the living church. We learned, too, that kind, tired, old Pastor Hsu was ready for retirement rather than more activity. The Methodist officials who were helping us in every way had left his transfer date up to us. Whenever we either felt capable of handling the situation ourselves or had Chinese personnel to meet the needs, they would appoint him to a smaller town where he could retire, and we could buy the church building for a nominal price.

This combination of circumstances resulted in an important decision, made December 26, 1948, and expressed thus in my diary: "We talked through the church situation again and decided to ask for the pastor's transfer. It's either faith or folly—faith, I am sure, though we have no ranks to choose from and not enough language skill ourselves to preach."

Surely the Lord rewarded our faith quickly that time! *The day after we mailed the letter,* we received a letter from the Methodists at Chengtu, telling us that Gordon Wang, a fine young seminary student whom we knew, would be willing to spend his "practice year" at Hochwan, if we were interested. "Interested" put it mildly; we were almost overwhelmed! In the Methodist yearly meeting at Chungking in January the transfer came about quietly and naturally, and to everyone's satisfaction. Gordon fitted in perfectly, and we never ceased to thank God for him. He was young both in years and in the Christian life, but his sincerity in serving the Lord caused both young and old to respect and love him. He was no great scholar, but he was an evangelist, and the latter was our first need in Hochwan.

Living with Gordon was James Lo, another answer to our prayers. James was only a high-school graduate, but he had always been quick to learn English; so his was unusually good. He helped in the work in many ways. Errands, teaching, writing out songs, translation, traveling companion—anything! He was a happy energetic young Christian who liked to share his blessings. One project he sponsored and thoroughly enjoyed was a series of literacy classes, teaching people who had never had educational opportunities to recognize enough characters to be able to read in the New Testament. Most of his students were inquirers from evangelistic meetings, but he never refused to teach anyone.

Also living in the parsonage with the boys and making a

home for them was a lady from North China whom they called Liu Ma. She loved the Lord and wanted to serve Him, and she felt this was how she best could do it. So she cooked and cleaned and was there to talk to the other women who dropped in. True, her dialect was so different that she was most difficult to understand. One time after she had gone on visitation a group of ladies came to ask whether it was true that if one attended church four consecutive times he received a bushel of rice! That was how much they understood her, and we did worse. We usually just nodded and smiled when she talked to us. One day we had the laugh on Christine when one of us heard her absent-mindedly agreeing to Liu Ma's statement, "You must have a great big loving heart to come so far and eat so much bitterness!"

Gordon and James worked with us for a year and a half, then it was time for them both to go back to school. As always, the Lord wonderfully provided for the needs of our group. A young seminary graduate from Chungking was willing to come. His wife had some training too, and was just as valuable as he. A third worker, a Bible woman named Miss Chia, spent several months with our church, but she left for her home before we did. John Chen and his wife were the two in charge when the church wisely severed connections with us later on. There was nothing personal in this decision; it was the only thing to do.

While the girls were walking in the country one day they made an important contact. A man whom they met and who seemed to want to talk turned out to be an official in the nearby orphanage. His first concern was whether he might send children with skin diseases and other minor ailments to us for treatment. Although the clinic plans were far from crystallized, they agreed. One thing led to another, and in a short time an invitation was given for someone to come each Sunday and hold Sunday school for the 130 children in the orphanage.

I wrote: "They are the most lovable youngsters you could

imagine. They go off like little torpedoes when they see us coming and run to spread the word. Then they assemble, each bringing his own tiny bamboo stool, and listen wide-eyed to the flannelgraph story about the life of Christ. One day Don knew their only ball was ruined; so he took them a new one. As he stood up to make a presentation speech, they caught sight of something round in his bag; so when he asked, 'What is the greatest gift the Lord ever gave to mankind?' they answered in one voice, 'A basketball!' " That door stayed open for many months, and before it closed those children knew much of God and His Word.

Another very early opportunity we had was to conduct English Bible classes. Under the Nationalist Government, the English language was a required subject in junior high and high school. More important, skill in English was required of anyone who expected to rise in government circles. Bank clerks, post-office employees, schoolteachers—all those and more had a great desire to learn better English. We simply had no time to teach English as a personal favor to them, but we did feel that English Bible classes would bring us excellent contacts and be worth-while investments of time. Invitations came almost faster than we could accept them. All five of us had classes in various high schools; some of us more than one. One principal told one of the girls that he hoped his pupils would "all become little Christmasses" as a result of these classes. We hoped so too!

It sounds almost dishonest when we tell our technique of teaching, but the truth is that it was the only thing we could do. Those youngsters just didn't understand English! At best they knew a few disconnected words and memorized sentences, but so far as conversational give and take was concerned, their English was just nil. The result was that if anybody was to learn anything, the class had to be about 90 per cent in Chinese and 10 per cent in English. Honestly, they got all the English they could absorb, and we were happy to see them understanding—in Chinese—the life of Christ in simple form, the Lord's Prayer, the Twenty-third Psalm, and other valuable Scripture portions and Bible stories. Everybody was satisfied!

On Sunday mornings before Chinese worship service began we conducted three English Bible classes, one for high-school boys, one for high-school girls, and one for adults. Pupils from these classes often stayed for preaching services, and we were especially happy later on to see someone who didn't have time for both services occasionally choose the Chinese "big worship," as it was called.

Sunday school was the next venture of faith, and again it grew so quickly that our facilities were sadly stretched. Ruth Bean was the chief sponsor of this effort, with all of us helping as we could. She wrote enthusiastically after the third week:

"Ever since we came to Hochwan, we've been saying, 'We must open a Sunday school.' After the arrival of our new pastor, Gordon Wang, and our helper, James Lo, we felt that we had adequate leadership and were ready to begin. Accordingly, we announced in the morning service that there was to be Sunday school at two o'clock that afternoon. All the children were urged to come and bring their friends.

"Two o'clock came—but no children! That didn't surprise us much, for no two people in Hochwan ever have the same time. We waited a little; then, not at all cast down, went out into the highways and byways to invite them to come in. All the tousle-haired, bright-eyed little friends who like to shout *How-bu-how!* (How are you?) at us as we walk down the street were soon gathered into the church—fifty of them! Most of them had never been inside before, and thought we would want them to give money.

"That was three weeks ago, and we have progressed from that beginning, for today we had over sixty-five present. You can imagine the motley crowd they are—some with hair in neat braids, rosy-cheeked, clean, and polite; others with bare, muddy feet, runny noses, hard to manage, but no less lovable. They love to sing and recite the memory verse, but they find it just as hard as do American children to sit still while a story is being told."

Sixty-five sounds like a good many, but ere long we had a hundred more than that, and at the peak almost two hundred more! They developed wonderfully from unmanageable scamps who had no idea why they came, into eager, orderly little friends who loved to learn more about their own heavenly Father. Of course, they weren't perfect, but whose children are?

Sunday-school teaching was the place where we could and did put our teen-agers to work. Often they knew little more than the children—they were that new in the faith—but they were willing to try, and Ruth did a splendid job of preparing them. Each week they met in teachers' meetings, where one teacher practiced telling the next Sunday's story while the others criticized and analyzed. The teachers learned more than the children, and it was very good for them.

Twice in our short history Ruth supervised solid weeks of Bible school, one in hot summer and the next one (she had learned her lesson!) in winter. If we except the well-qualified teachers, the wonderful materials, and the ideal equipment you have in America, we can say that our Bible schools were similar to any you might see in your local church! Again I will quote from Ruth as she wrote home after the first school:

" 'Calling all children! Calling all children! Only do not call too many, for fear we should not have enough classrooms, teachers, or materials to go around!' It was with such hopes and reservations that we opened our first summer Bible school in Hochwan.

"After seeing our Sunday-school attendance mushrooming from fifty to two hundred and fifty in five months, we had no doubt of our ability to assemble enough children for a week of Bible school. For various reasons we decided to make this first school a modest venture. As we had only two teachers we planned for two classes and ruled that total attendance be limited to a hundred children. But how enforce this limit in our church where hordes would push in if they suspected something special was happening? How devise a plan to reach children who did not already have opportunity to attend Sunday school? We felt a debt to the thousands in the city and its environs who have not yet heard the good news of salvation. We solved these ticklish problems by holding it in a village school outside the city wall. A number of the teachers of the Sa Ping Hsang School have come to our evangelistic meetings and Bible classes, and, as the principal was friendly, we had no difficulty in getting permission to use their school. Several days before opening, 'advertisements' were pasted in strategic places along Main Street, and on Saturday one of our teachers spent the afternoon registering interested pupils.

"On Saturday morning we had the first in our series of teachers' meetings. It was in these meetings that the two Chinese teachers, and Luella Gingerich and I as their assistants, laid plans, formulated policies, discussed teaching methods, and fashioned lesson plans. Neither James (our co-worker) nor Frances (a local convert) has had any teaching experience except that gained in our Sunday school. They are only beginning in the Christian life; their knowledge of the Bible, outside of Matthew or John, is pitifully meager; but they know the Christ to whom they have given their hearts, and they are convinced of the need to witness to His power. Day by day we assimilated the lesson content for the morrow, much as the children of Israel gathered the manna for their daily needs.

"Both from choice and necessity we built our course of six lessons around incidents in the life of Christ: from choice, because we felt that children totally ignorant of the God we worship would see Him only as revealed in Christ; from necessity, because all the flannelgraph materials we have are on the same subject. The worship period helped still further to clarify their understanding of the Son of God who became man, as Gordon Wang spoke to them on the 'I Am's' of Christ. Our teachers did a remarkably good job of emphasizing the focal points in these lessons, and, short as the time was, we trust and pray that the majority of children who attended regularly could follow the plan of the Father in sending His beloved Son into the world.

"The attendance was not as regular as we wished, but there was a goodly number who came every day. We were thankful that although we had almost a hundred children each day, we never had to turn any away. We were happy to include in our classes children who had never been to school, and while they could not read characters, they could nevertheless understand the Bible stories, memorize the songs and Scripture passages, and draw pictures. We were not unmindful to pray for the parents and the older villagers who came to look in the windows while the story was being depicted on the flannelboard."

Our frequent references to our use of flannelgraph remind me of a significant incident. Some friends were leaving China and we were planning to stay on. They called me to their home and showed me the many things they were disposing of. I refused the offer of a ten-wheeled truck, but clutched at a fifty-cent book of flannelgraph!

Evangelistic meetings were a never-ending opportunity in China, for the Chinese are a curious people, and always ready to take time to listen to something new. They are seldom in a hurry. So it was that we could easily fill the church in a few minutes each Friday evening, and Gordon could preach to them. We simply stood at the gate and sang. People stopped, the Chinese Christians explained to them that they were invited to a meeting, ushered them in, and the church was soon full to overflowing. I wish I could say that the conversions were in proportion, but that is not true. The Chinese were quick to listen but slow to accept. Many inquirers did stay after such services, some came back, a few clearly accepted

Christ. As in Christ's parable, the seed was sown, and surely some fell on fertile ground. God has promised that His Word shall not return unto Him void, but shall accomplish that which pleases Him, and we claimed that promise.

Other regular meetings which we occasionally took turns in leading were prayer meeting, Bible study class, and workers' meetings for our whole staff. Usually these were on a very small scale, and sometimes we felt discouraged at the slow growth we saw. On the whole though, we were an optimistic family. Maybe it was because our entire staff averaged 26½ years old. No, doubtless it was because God's hand was so definitely on us and His Spirit so clearly guiding us. We often sang together from our hearts:

"Bless Thou the gifts our hands have brought,
　Bless Thou the work our hearts have planned,
　Ours is the faith, the will, the thought,
　　The rest, O God, is in Thy hand."

7. House - Building Headaches

In February when the men made the final decision as to the field of Hochwan, they also chose a site for our future home. The property belonged to the Methodist Church and years ago had housed a girls' school. For a long time since, it had been used as an inn, with a number of shops on the street front. Besides rooms for overnight guests, there was space for a number of resident families. Everyone was living there for nothing or very little; so they naturally hated to hear that moving day was coming. They were clearly told in February that November 1 was the dead line, and we thought that certainly was ample warning. But upon our arrival in November we soon discovered that no one had moved or made any plans to move. The responsibility rested on the Methodists, for we had bargained to buy the premises empty, but the inconvenience was ours, for we wanted to occupy! Hence Don and Ed Knettler, the Methodist District Missionary, worked on the problem together.

They soon exhausted their occidental patience with the approved Chinese techniques of gently hinting or even having someone else do that. They told folks they must move, and soon! Slowly a trickle started, and eventually all but a couple of families were gone. With one man went all the wooden doors from his rooms; Don and Ed calmly searched out his new residence, found some of the doors, and had them brought back. The next-to-the-last tenant wasn't really a tenant. He had only an attic full of leather scraps from his shoemaking business, but he seemed to have no intentions of moving them; so the men climbed to this attic and started assisting him. It went off in good Chinese style, the renter doubtless raging inwardly but on the surface only protesting that he was troubling Don and Ed, and the boys throwing leather with great gusto, all the while smiling that it was no bother at all. We heard afterward that he never did forgive them; the wonder is that he didn't cause us trouble in the day of retribution. The last family developed a bad siege of measles, and in a number of weeks lost three children. Of course we didn't hurry them, but eventually they moved and the place was ours to begin on.

At first we tried optimistically to visualize this corner and that converted into something livable, but we weren't long in getting more realistic. Had we tried to live in those huge, dark, damp, dirt-floored rooms we would have had both tuberculosis and pneumonia the first winter. Some of the rooms extended all the way up to the high tile roof; others had a false ceiling of bamboo mats. The dust really came tumbling down when the rats ran across those mats! No room was sealed; rather, the walls all turned into open latticework about eight feet from the floor, opening either into the next room or the outside courtyard. We swallowed our pioneering instincts and decided to tear this more-than-hundred-year-old structure down and build a snug livable little home. The term "we" is purely editorial, for the job was Don's. It was a trying experience for him, what with pleasing four ladies who were always changing their minds, language barriers, no electricity or power tools, endless delays because of the difficulty of obtaining money for pay roll and materials, the continual feeling that he should be doing other things rather than this, and slow, unambitious workmen who took no particular pride in their work and seemingly cared more about how much they could get by with.

Don had had some previous experience in building, and embarked on this venture with typical Irish assurance. Before he was through, the dour, pessimistic Scotch half of his background, was dominating, and not without reason! But when he was through we had a lovely little home, too. When I first wrote home about it I used to describe it as looking like a train parked on a siding. Since we arrived in the States we learned an easier description. It looked much like that which covers the countryside from coast to coast—the popular motel!

The very first day of managing a carpentry crew opened Don's eyes to what he might expect. The foreman informed him that it was our responsibility to hire a cook for the men, though they all lived near by. Investigation soon proved that this was utterly false, but if Don hadn't inquired the foreman would have saved a nice amount of money during those months. We did furnish fuel, dishes and chopsticks, and the men ate three meals a day right there on the lot. The same afternoon along toward quitting time, Don learned a second lesson. He found men cutting perfectly good lumber into short lengths and putting them into baskets. Inquiry revealed that workmen were entitled to take scraps under a certain length home, and since the razing of the old structure had not yet yielded any such scraps, they were manufacturing some, out of our materials and on our time!

Several days went by, and an amazingly slight amount of work was accomplished. Investigation turned up two main reasons: The head carpenter, who was paid as a full-time worker on our job, was running another crew simultaneously and only spending half time on our job. And of his eight men, not the customary one but four were young apprentices, completely new at the trade. A young Chinese who worked with Don the first few months helped a great deal in solving these daily mysteries. He was no builder, but he was a zealous new Christian. His efforts doubtless saved us much time, money, and trouble.

It became a sort of guessing game—what surprise would this day bring forth? The next one came when Don met the afore-

5

mentioned cook slipping out the gate with a big load of charcoal. He admitted that he had been making it all the time, in our stove and from our wood, and selling it privately! A bit later Don came across one of the men doing his laundry during working hours.

Perhaps he could have learned to endure these endless tricks of the trade, but what Don could not endure was the poor quality of work being done. Two of the men had been assigned the job of building beds for the servants and the Chinese evangelistic workers. Assuming that they knew more about it than he did, Don didn't check until four beds were finished. When he stopped by to inspect the work, he found that the carpenters hadn't bothered to select good wood for the job; they had just picked up the first piece they laid hands on. To prove his point to them, Don struck a leg of each bed with the heel of his hand, and in each case it broke right off.

After a few more such demonstrations of poor workmanship and dishonesty, and since there was no indication of a desire on their part to do better, Don fired the whole outfit and started over—he figured he could get no worse help, and it might be better! This time he did get a much more satisfying group to work with. He admitted, too, that his blood pressure felt more nearly normal as he learned to lower his standards of perfection a bit. But to the end of the job, one of the most frequently heard phrases among the workmen was, "That's not far off," and Don's certain response was, "It can't be off at all. It's got to be the same!"

Ready-made furniture was expensive and not too well made; so we decided to have some made to order. By a rare stroke of diplomacy, Don persuaded all four of us women to agree on relatively uniform designs in beds, dressers, washstands, chairs, and built-in closets. Soon a special crew for furniture making was hard at the job. Don prepared rough drawings to indicate the processes involved, and pictures from a Montgomery Ward catalog helped the workmen visualize the finished product.

Because the head carpenter knew that we intended to paint or lacquer our own furniture, he was unconcerned about appearances, patching and plugging holes with great abandon. We genuinely liked what we eventually had, though, and took real pride in our newly furnished rooms.

When the clinic buildings and servants' quarters were finished, it was time to start on our own residence. Two more crews were added, stonemasons and brickmasons. The chow line assumed impressive proportions and Don was spending ten to fourteen hours a day on the job.

Up to this time, most of the material used had been salvaged from the buildings we had torn down. Although some parts had been very old, there was good lumber, brick, roof tile, and cut stone. Now, however, as we started the house, it was necessary to buy logs to be cut into lumber, bricks baked in local kilns, lime for plaster, and various other items. In China one doesn't call the lumberyard, ask the price, place the order, and expect prompt delivery. For instance, let me describe how Don got logs. He didn't go to any office; he went to a certain teahouse. The log merchant was there most of the day. Don was introduced to him, then joined him at tea, peanuts, and dried watermelon seeds. The unhurried conversation may have been about any subject except one—logs! Eventually one or the other of the men delicately approached the business at hand, and soon Don and the merchant were walking a mile or two up the river's edge to where the logs were stacked. Here the time-consuming bargaining proceeded in earnest. (It is described at length in another chapter.) Acceptable terms were finally reached, Don chose the logs he wanted and marked each one so that he could identify it later, the delivery fee was paid, and carriers started off to deliver them. The huge ones were carried by two or four men; the eight-foot logs were carried by individuals who bent 'way over and balanced the logs on their backs. When the logs arrived, the carpenter proceeded to ink guidelines on each side for the sawmen to follow, and of course a separate crew had to be secured to saw the boards. (Don't think all the union complications are on this side of the ocean!) It was a slow process, for their two-man saws were cut as strips from gasoline drums, teeth filed in, then tempered in sections. With such a poor grade of steel, a great deal of time was spent in sharpening saws, rather than cutting boards. After the boards were cut from eight-foot logs, they were invariably uneven and had to be planed a great deal. Imagine the amount of time consumed in preparing the tongue and groove flooring for our house, then doors, window frames, closets, and cabinets. Can you wonder why it took eight months to build a simple house?

Don was thankful for every tool he owned. Though he had no power tools, yet he did have equipment that saved hours of work. For instance, in the matter of boring holes, the Chinese carpenters had no other way than to use chisels for anything larger than nail size. A brace and bit would accomplish this in a minute, or course. The workmen never tired of gathering around each time Don opened his tool box. We only hope someone is utilizing those tools these days!

Some hardware was for sale on hardware street, but nails and most of our other needs were forged on blacksmith street. Glass was only sold by the pound, as were axheads, nails, hinges, and most metal products. After the first glass cutter broke eight of the nine panes he attempted to fit, Don hired a more skilled craftsman. It was a difficult task, for each pane was slightly curved.

After more than a year of bathing in wash basins, we were unanimously enthusiastic in our response to Don's suggestion that we order a bathtub. He had discovered the street where wooden buckets were made, and had asked whether they could make a large-sized model to our specifications. They could and did. He bound it with wire hoops and called in a lacquer-master to finish the outside in a handsome shining black. Chinese lacquer has the effect of high-powered poison ivy on many foreigners; so we didn't finish the inside! But how about plumbing? We girls only knew that we pulled the plug and the water ran out. Here is Don's description of where it went:

"Recalling that I had several old flashlights, I formed a plan. With my expansive bit I could drill a hole in the bottom of one end of the tub which would exactly allow me to screw the flared head of the flashlight case into it. Thus the water could drain into a large tin can below the floor. To this can I connected a bamboo pipe and waterproofed the joint with putty. So far so good, but a 45 degree angle had to be passed to lead the drain to the outside gutter. Again with the use of a swivel-head flashlight and appropriate soldering, I made the angle and joined on a second bamboo length to complete the job. Nails driven in the exposed end of the pipe insured against rats trying to creep in and surprise us."

Admittedly this narration has been mainly one of patience-trying incidents, but building was mainly that. There were happy relationships too, and countless opportunities to speak of and show forth the love of God. Sunday is no holiday in China, and the men expected to work on that day. We didn't want them to, yet felt it was not right to deprive them of a day's work which they could ill afford to miss. We reached a satisfactory agreement when we paid them the minimum daily wage for *not* working, and invited them to attend services at the church. Some came; some took an odd day's work elsewhere. On the night of our weekly evangelistic meetings, they always stopped work early, and many of them attended. There they heard the Gospel preached clearly in their own dialect. Only God can know the exact fruits of this endeavor, but we have faith in the power of God's Word to change men's hearts and lives. We had the joy of seeing the chief carpenter become a Christian, and because of that the latter working days were much more pleasant than the early ones.

The Chinese workmen, merchants and neighbors alike, were much impressed by the long sweaty hours of work Don put in side by side with his men. They had grown up in old China under the impression that gentlemen didn't get their hands dirty. Here was a college-trained preacher who was inevitably the dirtiest one of the crew at the end of each day! This was a language that meant something. Don, in turn, learned real appreciation for some of the craftsmen with whom he worked. Working with the simplest tools, a minimum of detailed plans, and limited physical energy, they toiled patiently and eventually produced what he was asking of them. My description of Don's continual checking on his crews may make him sound like a hard master. The Chinese workmen would agree with me in saying that he was not. They had a good employer and they knew it. He learned to adjust to and accept their oriental ways, and they displayed untiring good nature toward him, smiling broadly at criticism and even grinning sheepishly when surprised at some forbidden practice.

By the end of June, 1949, we had our house. It was gray brick, trimmed in painted green woodwork. Each of us had a bedroom; we shared a common dining-living room; there was a tiny kitchen, a back court for laundry, an outside toilet, ample storage space, and a cistern. We varnished our floors, painted our own furniture, and moved proudly into our handmade home. But then the heat of summer was upon us; so instead of taking a vacation *in* our new house, we took a vacation *from* it.

8. The Open Road

The only word which does not apply to travel in West China is "dull." Almost any other term would fit, what with roving bandits, narrow roads not meant for vehicles, springless rickshas already occupied by some of China's millions, slippery footpaths, swinging bridges, flash floods, no service stations, brakeless buses sailing downhill with the motor off to save gas, trucks so covered with "yellow fish" (extra passengers with whom the driver has private financial arrangements) that the driver can scarcely see out, roads blocked by heavy trailer loads being pushed or pulled by straining coolies, and curious country folk pushing close for a look at the high-nosed foreigners.

So it is that when anyone in West China travels for a vacation, the term implies more of the idea of "change" than of "rest." The summer of 1949 we jeeped from Chungking to Chengtu with our good friend Olin Stockwell. We were still impressionable then; so I wrote down the details, realizing that after a few more such ventures it would all seem quite commonplace. Here is that letter, in part:

"It was about 6:15 A.M. on the morning of July 7 that we set sail from Chungking. Along with Frank Cooley of the YMCA, and Olin Stockwell and Ed Knettler, Methodist missionaries, we set out for Suining, Ed's home. We hoped to be in early for supper; Olin could take care of a few business calls that night while we saw the school grounds and visited a bit; we would all turn in early, get a good start the next morning, and have supper in Chengtu. A lovely morning it was to travel—cool, cloudy, and the humidity must have been down to 90 for a change. The jeep was on its very best behavior, the heavily loaded trailer sailed right over the bumps, and life looked good. It was Don's twenty-ninth birthday and the first day of our vacation.

"And then it started to rain. There was nothing too unusual about that; it usually rains. But we noticed it particularly because the top few inches of the road immediately started melting, as well as because the outer circle of passengers got wetter and wetter as the rain came in the sides, through the top, and down the windshield of the jeep. Ready-for-any-thing-Olin was looking quite swank in an inherited poncho, but the wetter and muddier he got, the more he looked like something out of a Buck Rogers comic strip! About 2:30 P.M. we pulled across a bridge which looked suspiciously as though we might be the last ones over, and a bit later we were waved to a stop as we entered the next small village. 'You can't get across,' they announced cheerfully, and a few minutes later our men returned to verify the fact. The bridge just ahead was rapidly disappearing from sight. There were two alternatives: We could wait it out, which might be a few hours, or days, or weeks, or we could head back to another road several hours away, and try for Chengtu that way. The latter didn't appeal much, especially to Ed who was only a theoretical two or three hours from home, and to whom most of the stuff in the trailer belonged. A hasty look at the bridge a quarter of a mile behind us helped us decide; we couldn't have got out had we wanted to!

"And so we settled down to watching the water come up the road to meet us from both directions. I kept vaguely wondering where we would go when they met, but the only lady in such a calm company surrounded by even less excited Chinese, doesn't voice such questions. Instead I peeled peaches and fed them to these males who by turns were reading, sleeping, taking pictures, preaching, and wading. The water which was just covering the bridge when we pulled in was now rising rapidly. It was a marvelous opportunity to study the Chinese mind and its capacity to accept quietly anything and everything which comes in times of crisis.

"As the water crept down the street, the tenants were unhurriedly preparing their few possessions for the annual trip down the way. As the carriers ambled in with their shoulder poles and baskets, those to whose homes the water would come next stood idly by, watching the carriers load, and exchanging reminiscences about last year's flood and the one before that. In fact, it seemed to me that the most-discussed subject that day was not the flood at all, but the amazing fact of how few folk had eaten a noon meal! 'Did you eat today?' 'Not since morning.' 'My husband told me to get lunch, but who could stop to prepare food on such a day as this?' All this followed by much laughter and repeated dozens of times. The carload of foreigners was by this time of considerably greater interest than the rising waters, and it was only when the word came that houses were collapsing into the water that our rating slipped to second place. We were quite relieved to have a bit of fresh air as the crowds dispersed.

"Along about 5:00 P.M. the water stopped rising and we took heart. Probably the next morning and possibly that night we could get out—if a few remnants were left of that bridge when the water went down. One of the food shopkeepers finally dragged himself away from the fun long enough to get some rice and bean curd cooking and we had Don's birthday party without the cake. By then some of the first families on the street were moving back in and the waters were receding as rapidly as they had risen. The sides of the bridge, then the sidewalk stones, and finally the floor of the bridge itself was visible. But about that time we discovered that there was *another* bridge around the corner with much higher and swifter water than that which we had been watching; so the end was not yet.

"The water behind us had gone down, and several big ten-wheelers had roared in to join us in our wait; now one of them started up and took off over the newly washed bridge. In about five minutes they came lumbering back over our bridge in reverse and announced that it was too dangerous ahead. But our men, who had been watching the situation for hours, still felt we had a chance, and were only glad these big boys hadn't gone ahead and made bigger holes out of the washouts they were sure to find. So we pulled ahead over the first bridge and up onto the edge of the second. Then began the final speculation. It was well after 9:00 P.M. and quite dark. The result was that no two people saw or felt or judged alike. Frank came back to report that he had been all the way across the bridge with water only to his knees and had found no big holes with his bamboo probing stick. The words were no more than out of his mouth when Don came rushing up to contradict Frank's recommendation that we go. The piece of earth Don had been standing on had broken off into the river, and only quick jumping had saved his neck. At this point he handed me his watch to put in my purse, and I hastily thought of a friend whose husband drowned in China during their first term; she still wears his watch.

"A report from the crowd indicated something exciting, and as tall Ed glanced over the heads of the crowd he reported, 'There goes Frank down.' A few minutes later Frank came back, dripping wet and badly scratched to tell how the ground on which he and a Chinese were standing suddenly sank, and they had found themselves in a hole more than waist deep. This time Olin went to see for himself and came back to say that we were going over and right now. He felt we dared not wait. Now I was *really* scared because Olin is a man of great determination and not easily swayed. But Ed, who leans a bit to the cautious side, said bluntly that he thought it would be foolish to take any chances when so soon we would be able to see the bridge floor and be sure. Olin mercifully agreed, and we all relaxed. In a few more minutes the bridge was visible all the way across. There were washouts all the way over, but Olin measured the narrowest place with a stick and announced that we had a 'good three inches' to spare.

"Please bear in mind that this bridge had no sides, the water had been rushing both under and over it at terrific speed, and no mortal could possibly know what the condition of the interior of it was. But this particular mortal had a pretty good idea of what it *could* be, and somehow couldn't work up a great deal of enthusiasm at Olin's magnificent clearance of three inches between the river, on one side, and a soft, ragged, undermined, deep mudhole on the other. I shed my shoes and Don led me across the bridge to the far side where I fixed myself firmly to a big pole. I knew my legs were not to be depended on. The scene that followed is a vivid but not too pleasant memory. The jeep started up, turned on one feeble light, and moved onto the bridge. Dancing along like some sort of water nymph came Frank. He was running backward, barefooted, on the utter edge of the bridge, holding a flashlight and urging Olin closer and closer. I hope it is the nearest thing I ever see to a mermaid, and he surely didn't do a bad job of looking the part. With his thick crop of red hair, white shirt and white shorts, wildly beckoning Olin, it seemed to me, to plunge right off the bridge into the swirling waters below— it was pretty hard to imagine for a few minutes that he had Olin's best interests at heart. Of course the fact of the matter was that he had but recently emerged from that pothole on the other side, and knew that the stone edge of the bridge was a lot safer. But Olin was leaning out the left side, driving just as close to the hole as he could. I don't really think he even saw Frank's light. Then it was all over, and the onlookers were saluting Olin and Company with the spontaneous cheers which are a Chinese specialty at such times. We were back in the jeep, the moon came out, the rains had stopped, and the roads were drying up the way they do only in Szechwan

Province. As we buzzed along toward our destination Don remarked that it was like the calm after the storm in Beethoven's Pastoral Symphony.

"It got later and later, and it seemed we flew faster and faster over those rough roads, steep grades and inclines, and sharp switchbacks. Ed knows his home country and he kept saying, 'This is a steep downgrade coming, Olin,' or 'Look out for a bad corner up here,' but somehow Olin didn't seem to hear him. At least that's what we thought till we pulled into Ed's about 2:30 A.M. and practically went right on over the compound wall and into the moat beyond it. 'Hold her,' yelled Ed, to which Olin replied, 'You hold her, brother. I can't. She hasn't had one iota of brakes since we crossed that bridge four hours ago.' Seems he hadn't wanted to disturb our poor tired minds after our recent harrowing experiences!

"Morning came a lot too early that Friday and while Olin sandwiched in a lot of business items, Don took the jeep to the local service station. They fixed the lights, brakes, checked the oil, radiator, and springs, or so they said. By ten o'clock we were ready to leave and the sun was really beating down. There had been so much rain that the shorter road was impassable and we set off on the longer route. In by midnight, was our fond hope.

"We hadn't been long on the road till 'ping,' we heard a piece of metal fly off our underpinning and glance off the rocks. No wonder—such roads! We laughed as we read on the metal plate fastened to the dashboard that the maximum speed for the jeep was thirty-three miles per hour. I don't suppose we ever did above fifteen and most of the time a good deal below that. But about that lost piece—it was just the first of three springs that were to break. We stopped, jacked the jeep up, and fastened in half of an old tarp from the trailer. I am the wrong person to ask how a piece of cloth substitutes for a spring, but we soon were on our way. Number two went out in a village; so we watched with interest as Olin repaired it with three pairs of locally made grass sandals. The third spring was fixed the same way and eventually when we totaled up we seemed to have nine pairs of sandals plus the original hunk of canvas. The bumps were harder and the driving had to be more careful, but we kept moving.

"Now it was Frank's turn to drive, and he announced that the brakes had again utterly disappeared but we careened along our way, dividing kilo signs by eight and multiplying by five and honking the horn at all comers. The vehicles were few and far between—likely all held up somewhere by floods, and the country folk were still frightened enough to run at the sound of a jeep. In the early afternoon Olin pulled into a little village and called to the young seminary-student passenger we had picked up in Suining, 'Go and buy us some wine.' 'Wine?' echoed the lad. 'Maybe you mean alcohol.' No, it was wine that Olin meant, and while waiting for the boy to bring it he disappeared under the jeep for his periodic tour of inspection. Then he took a hammer, somehow managed to seal off the front wheel where the brake fluid was leaking out, took off the plate on the floor of the car, borrowed a bit of bamboo from a bystander, and proceeded to pour the contents of the pewter wine pitcher into the tube where the brake fluid had once been. It was new to us but it certainly worked, and soon we were on our way, with brakes!

"By this time the radiator had settled pretty well into a feeding schedule; it seemed to need attention every seven to ten minutes. The battery also took nourishment quite often, the oil was leaking nicely, and even the passengers were pretty well on a liquid diet. We were no longer stopping for food, but only to swallow huge gulps of boiling water with powdered coffee when one of our forced stops happened to be near a tearoom. The starter often stuck, and sometimes couldn't be rocked loose, in which event the whole front end had to be taken apart. The generator was not working because the fan belt was too loose; so that needed frequent tightenings. The battery cable was always jarring loose from the bumps, and we were eternally having to stop to fill the water cans.

"It got so that every stop was about like pulling into the modern American service station; the only difference was that here the passengers were the attendants. After a few hours' practice it was a thing of beauty to behold the efficiency of our stops. Men crawling everywhere, pouring liquids into every orifice, roping, checking, tightening, loosening, sweating, running, jumping on as we started, and catching their breath till the next stop. Sort of like a well-trained football team, with nobody even calling signals. The horn and tires were about all that were not undergoing treatment and I am perfectly sure that anyone who would have ventured to mention either of those items as possible candidates for failure would promptly and justly have been hit squarely over the head with a wrench.

"All along the way the roads were unspeakably bad. There had been much rain and high water and nowhere was more than the bedrock left; sometimes only part of that. We tried to combine optimism with realism as we grudgingly kept advancing the hour which we considered the earliest possible for arrival. As we pulled out of Mienyang after our 8:00 P.M. peach and cup of coffee, and saw the 134 kilos to go, my mind seized on 2:00 A.M. as a new goal. But when about 9:00 P.M. it was dark enough for lights and we discovered that we had none, nor would we have, my hopes waned. None of us thought for a moment of stopping. Instead we thanked the good Lord for a perfect moon and cloudless sky. Indeed under different circumstances that ride could have been quite romantic and poetic, for all was silver and silhouette. But the novelty wasn't long in wearing off, and it became one of the most weird journeys you can imagine. Those hundreds of shadows—every one was a possible bad hole in the road and might finish our trip. Those innumerable patches of light after darkness—every last one looked like a stretch of water across the highway.

"Eleven o'clock, twelve, one, two, slowly but surely we were getting nearer home, roaring our muffler-less way through the absolute quiet of the countryside, punctuating our progress with our wordless, well-ordered stops. On one stop Don found a rider on the trailer, and close behind a couple of his cronies approaching. Doubtless the leaking radiator was a blessing that time, for had we not stopped and gone for the water can, our baggage, piece by piece, would have been tossed off into waiting hands along the way.

"At 3:00 A.M. we met with what we thought was an impossible situation. A firmly locked walled city, and no road around. And they would not open the gate. Frank and the young Chinese student argued with them endlessly but to no avail. Finally Olin hoisted his long weary self out from under the wheel and joined their conference. A few minutes later he came back and informed me that he had appealed to their respect for the weaker sex. By then I was genuinely ill, and he had told them so. We were all sick from no rest, no food, rough travel, and nervous tension. The skeptics came close with their flashlights to see for themselves, and I'm sure I looked as ghastly as I felt. The appeal may have helped, but the silver Frank showed the man doubtless helped more. Our hopes rose to see the hesitant gatekeeper take his job in his hands and unlock the city gate. In we rolled, he riding with us to explain for us to the gateman at the other end.

"And now this sounds like a story taken too far, but it is true that at the other end of the city that watchman would not open for love or money or a sick lady either. He just wouldn't take the chance. The first man didn't want to give the money back; so he worked on the problem. After another round of whispered conferences we were no further. Frank was adamant. He tried to be polite, then helpless, then firm, and then he blustered. He naturally met with no success in requesting to speak to the higher city officials; so he paced the street below their window (all this at 3:30 A.M.) and inquired in tones that echoed for blocks just who was going to be responsible for my death. I began to wonder myself! Then came another whispering group of well-wishers who agreed that for a price the gate could be opened and the jeep and trailer pushed out—not start the engine, understand, but push them silently. Wonderful, excellent, perfect! We could leave! But now the unkindest cut of all. As the gate squeaked open, it was apparent to all concerned that even with Olin at the wheel, the jeep could never squeeze between all the huge army trucks that were parked at crazy angles outside, waiting for dawn.

"Maybe that was the climax. Because after that we just slept for an hour—three of us on parts of our sole bedding roll on the ground, and two in the jeep. Then came another hour of moving and starting and jockeying of the trucks and after that another three hours of painful awful driving over the worst roads yet. We were sore, we were sick, we were hungry and thirsty. I hated that can of cold water; I hated those leisurely old buffalo who had just finished a good night's sleep and were sticking their ugly faces 'way down into cool, refreshing water; I hated every kilo sign along the way; I think I hated everything but the temperature indicator on the dashboard. I could hardly wait till it got up past 200 so that we could stop for a minute—riding was simply agony. And so it finally ended about 8:30 A.M., this fifty-hour drive with maybe five hours of sleep.

"The world knows no gentler hands to fall into than those into which we fell, and the process of sleeping our way back to the surface, of getting our eyes to focus and our legs to function, was almost fun. As soon as I was anatomically able to type (I only type sitting down) I felt this thing must be written and quickly. Because everybody who hears it has a better story to tell, about his trips, and it makes me ashamed of myself for thinking it was anything special."

Row upon row of idols in a Buddhist temple.

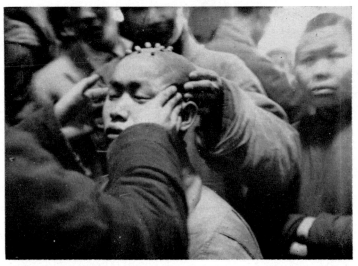

Incense being burned on the head of a young acolyte being initiated.

5-A

LEFT. *Tribes people from Sikang Province. They wear goat skin garments and shoes.* RIGHT. *Nurse Julia displays sign advertising the clinic.*

A covered bridge like the one which cracked the top braces off the truck which was taking us to Behludin.

Hochwan water front scene.

A lean-to home like those in which the displaced persons live for months at floodtime.

The opening of the waters at Kwanhsien. Note the section of the dam which has just been pulled loose.

Striking students on West China university campus vote on an issue at a mass meeting.

Making boards from logs for our home.

Stonemasons at work on our lot with their crude tools.

A partial view of the home we built in Hochwan.

Another view of our home.

LEFT. *Planting rice in rows.* RIGHT. *Threshing rice.*

*Plowing under water to prepare the field for transplanting of rice.
The water buffalo is owned by several families.*

The soldiers who came to defend us from bandits.

Orphans who came to the clinic for medical treatment.

9. Now We Are Six

A short but very thrilling chapter should concern the wonderful way in which Eugene Blosser arrived in China to claim Luella Gingerich for his wife. She was a member of our original group, but he was still in college. He was appointed to China later on, and there was much suspense and uncertainty about his actual coming. In the summer of 1949 we persuaded Luella that she had better go to India to wait for him. That seemed the best route for him to come, then both of them come through China's back door if it were still open. She left us, all properly farewelled, but wrote a few days later from Chungking that she had changed her mind and was coming back! Nothing surprised us, and surely we were *almost* as anxious as she was to have our mission family number six instead of either five or four.

In late August of 1949 Eugene sailed on a freighter bound for Hong Kong, and Luella flew out that far to meet him. She was interested in the quickest reunion possible, and then a dash back into rapidly closing China. Consequently when Eugene opened a letter from her at a stop in the Philippines, out fell a clipping from the Hong Kong paper announcing their intention to wed!

He arrived on September 15, and on the nineteenth they were married in Hong Kong. They were happy to have Daniel and Rosalie Stoltzfus, new MCC workers who traveled to Hong Kong with Gene, for attendants. (Later these same friends welcomed and entertained our whole group by one's and two's as we wended our way out of China.) None of us could attend the wedding, but according to their pictures and their glowing story it must surely have been a lovely ceremony.

After a week's honeymoon on the bay, they flew to Chungking, where I had the joy of representing our group in meeting them. Esther and Olin Stockwell, then living in Chungking, drove me to the airport, and we all felt extremely happy to see the Blossers land on Szechwan territory.

The very day after we arrived Luella and I went down to the hospital and hired Julia, the Chinese nurse who would be replacing Luella in the clinic. Another story I can't resist telling happened on that Chungking visit, while I was waiting for the Blossers to fly in. Over the week end the Stockwells and I were invited to tour an institution administered by some people we knew. We arrived in a pouring rain, but they wanted us to see it all; so we sloshed around from building to building, getting wetter and wetter. By the time we came to their home we looked like something that had come up a drain. We three sat shivering in soaked seersuckers while our absent-minded hostess (an American) excused herself for a hot bath and came back in a *formal*, up-hair-do, jewels, and golden slippers! We, her only guests, damply joined her at a lovely crystal, linen, and candlelight table for dinner. We tried to refrain from snickering and sneezing, and barely succeeded only by strictly avoiding each other's glances.

When we were about to take off for Hochwan we sent the Board a cable, saying "entering the promised land," but like the children of Israel, we were delayed a bit. My bright idea of taking a bus to Peipei—halfway home—and then catching the steamer there, didn't pan out. Not my fault, but we missed the boat just as surely as though it had been! They said to come by seven; that was when the sale of tickets started. But when we got there at a quarter till, the tickets were sold out. By the time we got on a bus it was 10:30 A.M., and the boat was nicely past Peipei when we pulled in. We were very anxious to get home that night, but it was raining, a wooden boat wouldn't risk the rapids, chair carriers couldn't arrive, and we knew we couldn't walk thirty miles before dark. So we reconciled ourselves to a stopover in Peipei, and I headed for the telephone office, not even knowing whether there was one. There was, and ere long I was telling Christine our sad story. Of course we didn't have a phone, but I simply said they could call any Hochwan foreigner to the Hochwan telephone office. There are advantages to belonging to a rare species, you see. . . . We had both UNESCO and missionary friends in Peipei, and they hospitably shared us overnight and the next day.

It was a most awfully happy home-coming next night when the steamer pulled in. The church family and many other friends were there, and together we rejoiced at the fulfillment of our hopes and prayers. It was really something, for all we saw or heard about those days was people *leaving*, but here came Gene as calmly as you please, right through red tape and passport refusals and all the rest. We needed him much, and the Lord knew it. Something like this meant a lot to the faith of our new Christians. They had been praying about it too, and such a dramatic, romantic episode made a bigger impression on them than the daily little things. A day later we entertained about sixty friends at a combination welcome and open-house in our new home. After feeding our guests tea, cake, and cookies, we turned them loose in the house, and it was not only look *at*, but look *in* and look *under*. There was no stone left unturned. Their biggest disappointment, I think, was in Gene and Luella's bed! A Chinese wedding bed is about like a young apartment or a snug little bungalow, and they really rushed to see what our honeymooners would have. A simple roughly made bedstead, a lumpy camel hair mattress, not even one embroidered hanging to ask the gods that their marriage be blessed with children—it was quite a letdown, I'm sure.

We greatly enjoyed a month of being six around the table

and the organ. A final sign that Eugene really was meant for Hochwan; he sings tenor, the missing part in our quartet! Don really enjoyed the companionship of a man, after so many months of all women.

Soon the Blossers were off for school in Chengtu, supposedly for six months, then for a year. Finally when it became perfectly clear that they would never receive permission from the new government to come back to our station, they reluctantly left China. Philip Eugene was born on September 14, 1950, and they left China the following January. As someone commented later, "Eugene certainly had a lot of adjustments to make in his first year—a new land, a new wife, and a new baby." He made them well.

Such experiences could make one discouraged, bitter, and pessimistic, but the Blossers never questioned God's will. They seized on many opportunities for Christian witness in Chengtu, with students, servants, and English Bible classes. And as I write, they are waiting visas to enter a new field of work.

10. Clinic Contacts

One of the early stories circulating after our arrival said that all those barrels of freight contained the fixings for a shiny western-style hospital! The fact that there was no doctor among us didn't alter the case, for all foreigners knew how to heal disease, and wasn't Luella a nurse?

Our modest little clinic must have been quite a letdown to those who dreamed such dreams, but we thought it was fine. Part of the old buildings in front were remodeled according to Luella's specifications and used to house this project. A large room opening onto the street also doubled for a class-room—literacy, English Bible, or Sunday school—but on clinic day it was the waiting room. Here it was that the crowd pushed in when the door was unbarred, and clamored for numbers indicating who was to be seen first and next. On one occasion they actually broke the door, and on more than one they almost crushed the number-giver. Inside was a room where Luella met the patients, a tiny drug room, and adjoining was a bedroom for the Chinese nurse we hoped eventually to add to our group.

Even before the clinic rooms were ready, Luella was giving some treatments, especially to the little orphans. One small boy had an old gangrenous wound on his heel which had wait-ed too long already. She decided it must be cleaned up; so Don helped her rig an operating table on the back veranda at the German ladies' house where we were living, and they proceeded. The boy took it all fine, but the surgeon and her assistant didn't do so well. It was intensely hot, they hadn't been near anything like that for a long time, and they loved the boy. The combination resulted in first Don, then Luella, trying to faint! Christine was requested to brew strong coffee, and soon they were on their feet again. There's a sad ending to that story. The little fellow got involved in some trouble at the orphanage and ran away. Without treatment his bad infection must surely have taken his life—we never heard of him again.

The opening of the clinic brought a whole new circle of friends, and another excellent opportunity to show Christ's love. We always had tracts and Scripture portions on display in the waiting room and someone there to talk to the patients about them. Often patients came whose trouble was more unhappiness than organic, and it was a joy to tell them of One who loved them. There were no psychiatrists among us, but we did have the message of peace to give.

Luella's letter summarizes the first months of clinic activity thus:

"The clinic was finally opened April 1, two afternoons a week. We saw and treated 841 persons from then till July, but only averaged about forty per afternoon. The rest were seen outside of hours, or before the clinic was officially opened. Clinic afternoons usually required three of us, and we all came home completely exhausted. Patients crowded, pushed, and shoved to get in the door first, whole families tried getting into clinic on one ticket, and every time I stepped into the street it seemed someone was asking to have their *bins kanned* (illnesses treated). Christine acted as chief pharmacist, preparing the solutions and dispensing the drugs, and Dorothy and Ruth took turns in acting as hostess and treasurer, making the charges and trying to reckon with cash, silver, and bills of half-million-dollar denominations, all in the same day. I attempted listening to the patients' complaints, formulated a diagnosis if possible, if not, gave them the medication that seemed to nearest fit their vague complaints. Sometimes it was worm medicine, or soda mint; these two always seemed to produce wonderful effects. Whereas Dorothy used to allow her stomach to turn somersaults when we talked of smelly cases, she now has become an efficient assistant. When the family had its rounds of immunizations, she effectively administered the needle to me (after practicing on a fresh apricot!), and gained enough self-confidence that she almost considered setting up a private practice on the street to compete with the local practitioners who are so famous for their 'needles.' Most of the patients are able and glad to pay for their medicines, which we dispense at cost, but sometimes we get really bad cases that have no money, and it is a pleasure to treat them and see them respond to it. They are always so grateful."

We learned early that the Chinese are perfectly willing to mix their religions, hoping for some good from each. Often at a funeral ceremony representatives of two or three major religions might be present (and the Christian minister might be invited!) in an effort to secure the greatest good for the deceased. When the clinic opened, we discovered that they are just as prone to mix their medicines; so the first question before giving any "western" medicine was to ask what Chinese medicine they already were taking. The two couldn't safely mix, of course. There was in our immediate neighborhood almost every sort of medicine man, and one could have anything for a price—roots, herbs, pickled snake, ground-up monkey bones, or an endless variety of injections. Not few were the cases we met where children were blinded or otherwise maimed for life because they "ate mistakenly" or "injected mistakenly" of Chinese medicine. I remember one week when we saw a whole series of children covered with huge sores. They had supposedly been vaccinated for smallpox but whatever was given surely had a violent reaction on the poor little tots.

One of the health reforms of the new government was to see that everyone had annual immunizations. Some wouldn't have been needed annually except that the authorities had not yet devised an accurate system of record keeping. At various intervals we would see them giving injections or immunizations on the street or at the river front to everyone boarding the steamer. Fortunately we missed their shooting days—I didn't relish the idea of being stuck with the same needle which had already served somebody else. They changed after every third person!

Another custom I rebelled at even watching was a very common one. If a child was sick, the mother would lay it across her knees and pluck, pluck, pluck at the skin on its throat until there was a red welt there, about like a blood blister. This was supposed to draw the blood away from the afflicted part of the body. Adults would do it to themselves, of course.

Another indication that a person was not ten parts well was a cloth bound tightly around his head. I remember listening to a Chinese doctor friend gently chiding her patients about this old custom. "What's wrong," she would ask, "got a hole in your head?" The women would smile at themselves, but they didn't discard the cloth.

I am no pharmacist, but I do remember that the medical preparations were interesting to watch. With the help of a Chungking doctor, Luella had chosen basic supplies which she felt competent to dispense. Then it was a process of mix-your-own. Cough syrup? Cook the syrup, add the medicine. For children? Dilute it thus and so. Powders? Crush the pills and cut the pile in tiny squares to be wrapped separately. Instructions? Labels? Useless; most patients can't read. Every how many hours? No clocks. So it was verbal instructions, repeated and told back till we were satisfied that they understood. In the beginning we must have given some rare instructions! The words for "sore," "boat," and "bed" are much alike to a foreign ear. And I, for one, could seldom differentiate between "oil" and "medicine." I confess that often I must have told people to jump in their boats and rub some oil on their beds—how much worse than that it was I cannot tell!

There were no dull moments and many satisfied customers. They were particularly satisfied with our prices, for we made no effort to profit from them. Our goal was that the clinic might break even; so we calculated medicine costs in U.S. prices when we bought them, scaled it down to pennies or fractions thereof, and multiplied it over each day when we gave medicine, according to the current rate of exchange. I recall one hopeless old man who wobbled up and down the street on two sticks. He refused the verdict that we could not help him, and wouldn't go home until he got medicine. Finally in despair the Chinese nurse gave him enough harmless soda mint to last ten days. Next day he was back, saying it tasted so good he ate it all that night, and wanting more! Among the most pitiful and maddening cases were the tiny babies brought in by grandmothers or other relatives.

"What a nice baby."

"Yes, but he won't eat!"

"Does the mother have milk?"

"Yes, but he just takes it in his mouth and doesn't swallow it."

"Can't he swallow?"

"I guess not."

"How old?"

"Five days."

"Who delivered him?"

"I did."

"What did you use to cut the cord?"

"A cracked tile from the roof." (Or a sharp-edged cracked bowl, or her teeth.)

Another case of lockjaw in the last stages, with nothing in our power to do except stress again the importance of sterilizing equipment.

Eugene and Luella were with us for a month after their marriage then in order that Gene might study under the best conditions, they went to Chengtu. We hired a Chinese nurse who chose the English name Julia. She was a prize, and just one more on the long list of blessings God gave us. She ranked at the top of her graduating class, and the hospital where she had trained was eager to keep her. She didn't know any of us, and we offered her less than half the hospital salary, but she packed her roll of possessions and came with us. She had a few weeks of working with Luella to gain confidence, then she took over the clinic. She had professed to be a Christian when we interviewed her, but some weeks after her arrival at Hochwan she quietly stood at the invitation following an evangelistic sermon, thus signifying her desire to accept Christ. From then on she was a much more valuable part of our family, for she was eager to help in children's meetings, ready to speak for Christ in the clinic, and had a whole new outlook on life. She was one of the few who "finished the course" of Don's instruction class, and was baptized by him before she left us.

With Luella's going, some of the clinic fascination was gone, for the Chinese traditionally had more confidence in a foreigner. Both Julia and Christine felt that it would be a real service to the town if some course of instruction in general health, nutrition, disease prevention, etc., could be offered. We invited the mayor and others for tea, and after filling them full of foreign cookies and cakes which they dearly loved, presented the idea. In fact, we went wholly Chinese that day and had a Chinese friend there to present it for us. The idea struck them favorably, and soon Christine and Julia were preparing the series of lessons. Chinese families were organized in groups of 100, and the government arranged for this series to be presented to representatives of each family, a district at a time, with required attendance. This service continued until the government changed hands.

Another "extra" offered through the clinic was our baby-washing service. Some born in the fall have no bath till spring. Others with skin diseases especially needed extra bathing. The mothers were extremely enthusiastic and grateful. Here's what I said one day after we had bathed forty of them:

"Today was baby day and great fun. Julie and I wash babies all afternoon, and Christine is our 'front' woman. She talks to the mothers outside, hands out numbers, and sees that they get the babies undressed and ready before their turn comes. When the crowd is the largest Julie takes time out and teaches them a lesson on a practical level which they can remember and apply. It is a gratifying investment of time to turn the smelly little imps into clean, pink, powdered little dears. We wash heads and all, of course, which horrifies some of them. They insist on saying we use 'medicine water,' and all marvel at the fact that we use a clean boiled cloth and towel for each baby! Many of them have scabies. We burn wine in the pan after every bath, and finish off the treatment with a dusting of bean powder out of an old cinnamon can! We weigh them each time on the scale E. gave us, and it thrills the mothers to watch the charts climb steadily. Yesterday the mother of a four-month-old I was bathing told me it was the baby's first bath, and that's not uncommon. Two other mothers said they'd like to bathe the babies at home, but their mothers-in-law had 'old brains' and thought it was dangerous to bathe them; so they sneak off to the clinic twice a week. I don't know how they explain the loss of garlic flavor to grandma!"

Some mothers were extremely slow to accept our advice. I remember one who brought a poor rash-covered child wearing a tightly woven hair necklace. Of course his prickly heat was spreading from there, and I suggested she take it off. Next week it was still there, and he was still scratching. This time Julia told her it should come off. Yes, yes, she would. The third week Julia told her she couldn't bring the poor thing back again until that necklace was gone. All right, all right. "In fact," said Julia, picking up her scissors, "I'll just cut it off for you." At this the woman quickly picked up her child, exclaiming, "No, no! The child must be up in a tree when that is taken off!" Neither of us knew what sort of charm it was, but it meant something important to her superstitious beliefs.

Most people came to the clinic for medicine, but some came *with* medicine! Foreign medicine was greatly respected by the Chinese, and was very expensive. When someone had money to invest, he was safe in buying a sealed, genuine bottle of foreign pills. But what to do with them? It was not unusual for us to entertain some well-dressed merchant who would pull out such a bottle and ask us to read to him what it said, and tell him when to use it! There was no bothering with prescriptions in our town—all one needed was the cash, and he could buy one or a bottle of any pill the druggist had, be it sulfa or sleeping pills.

When people came begging we usually tried to have our Chinese colleagues talk with them, for they could spot a fake much more easily than we could. Once in a while, though, the gullibility of the Chinese was amazing. A man came to the clinic one morning with a huge purple growth on his face which he reported had appeared in twenty days. Julia was amazed, and called for Christine to come and see. Christine was no doctor, but she knew that man could only be helped by surgery. She suggested he go to the hospital. Julia immediately felt sorry for him, and thought we should help, but we could hardly give him a covering letter assuming all responsibility. That just wasn't done in China. I have seen beggars lying on the street in real need of help, but no one dared touch them for fear he'd have a lifetime burden the moment he did. The man now got quite emotional; he just couldn't leave until he was helped. He also got hungry; so Julia cooked him some noodles. As long as she was feeding him he was just fine, but whenever anybody questioned him he got a type of spasm. Julia was overcome with sympathy and called Gordon, the evangelist. He, too, felt we must do something, and the man sat on. Christine had long since concluded that he was a fake, but she felt for Julia's and Gordon's sake she must withhold her judgment a bit. Time wore slowly on until finally it was late afternoon. At long last the Chinese workers agreed that we should give him a certain amount of money for rice and pay for carriers to take him home. Christine made these arrangements and finally came into our living room to relax.

Not more than ten minutes later the quiet was broken by two extremely angry young friends, Gordon and Julia! Gordon had followed the man down the street, saw his carriers put him down, and when Gordon caught up with them he was trying to get their fees back from them. They told Gordon he'd lived in Hochwan for years, and they'd never known him when he didn't have this growth. He was just a professional who had found some tenderhearted easy marks!

11. Language in Action

I had grown up with Midwest American English, and was increasingly fascinated by the many interesting versions of the English language we met in China. My stomach turned a little at first when a Chengtu friend asked, in English-English, "Would you like your eggs scrambling?" but we soon mastered the frame and I could ask with a straight face if Don wanted his hair cutting or his water bottle filling.

When the Countess and Barbara, our first Hochwan neighbors, went home to Germany in 1949, their work was taken over by their German colleague Irmtrud von Haugwitz, and Thali Anderson, a Swedish girl. Our close companionship with that household continued, and we added Swedish-English to the German-English we'd been learning. They slept in payamas, went up very early in the morning, and washed their faces in animal-ware basins. We got along famously at understanding each other. I remember one day when we were canning peaches after they'd thought the season was finished. Asked Irmtrud, "Have you then a friend found who has longer peaches?"

Then began the long line of English-speaking Chinese friends. We used to be amused at some of their *faux pas* until my mother reminded us of how much funnier we doubtless sounded to them. She was right, and we never ceased to marvel at and appreciate their self-control, patience, and kindness as they helped us without laughing at us. Our mistakes could fill many a page, but they mostly weren't even close enough to correct to be laughable. I'll list a few mild examples, to comfort any student of a foreign language who might be reading this chapter.

In language school one of us apologized to the teacher for being late. "My nose is so big I just walk slowly," she said. It was, of course, her shoes, not her nose, that retarded her progress.

One day we had French toast with lemon sauce for dessert because the bread ordered was "fried" instead of "ginger."

One evening we understood the foreigner leading prayer meeting to suggest that before we pray we should vomit a few special prayer requests.

Then there was the day when through a language misunderstanding we paid for incense to be burned at our well before the coolie climbed in to clean it out! When we happened by it was too late.

By simply reversing two syllables, one of us prayed earnestly in public that God would bless us, His "daughters," rather than "children."

One of us, to her embarrassed horror, heard herself complaining to an innkeeper that she didn't have enough courage to sleep in the bed he provided. What she meant to say was that there weren't enough sheets, and a puff of air made all the difference.

Some of our Chinese friends spoke exceedingly well. One difficulty they all have is to differentiate between "n," "l," and "r." For instance, one friend had only one English word which she couldn't pronounce clearly. She *couldn't* say "rural"—it always came out "ruler." Another example of the N-L-R difficulty would be Mr. Pig's remark that he had been reading a "lover." We figured out eventually that it was a "novel." His favorite trick was to try French on us, and without saying it *was* French! We were all embarrassed when that happened. One night as he was leaving, he sang out "bone so well," and finally had to come back and tell us that it was "good evening" in French, *bon soir*!

Our favorite of them all was William, an English teacher in a local high school. His courage knew no bounds, and his English was not to be corrected. Other friends always begged us to correct them; not so William. He wouldn't take a correction if we did give it. He "will did my best-ee," and that was good enough. He loved to come and talk to us forge-iners. One time he invited Don to his "newly whited chamber" (whitewashed room) to "take sugar" (eat candy). He and his friends often played their mouth-oranges. He had a friend whose dog had round feathers, and another whose profession was selling the feathers of the pig. (In Chinese the word for feather, fur, bristle, and any hair except that on the head is the same—*mao*—as in the new chairman's name!) One of his colleagues, Wellington, came with him one day to discuss his problems. Early in life his parents had arranged a marriage for him. Now the time had come, and when he refused to go through with it his father came after him. Complained Wellington, "About my finance, she has studied very few. I feel no affection with her."

William found someone to feel affection with, and was married. As the day drew near for their first child to be born, he philosophized much. "I want to give my baby a softly. For my part, I know not why the bor-ji-us must suffer." Don agreed to help give this baby a softly by making a cradle for it. The child arrived early, and William wrote hastily:

"Dear McCammon, May you excuse me on my unpoliteness. At here you can't imagine how puzzling I am. My wife just birth a baby boy last night. I haven't one minute to sleep or rest till now time. Our bed had many bed bugs, it is a great troubling for our little baby, so we are very want you can help us in this way to make little bed for us. With so much thanks and wishes to you and your wife.

"If the bed shall be finished, you may announcing the boy Chin Wen-Chih who is living just before you gate, a son of a Chinese medicine merchant and the relative of my wife. How is your idea? My good Friend, Truly yours." The sweet little white cradle was soon on its way, not even slightly resembling the section of black stovepipe it was made from.

When the baby was a month old, the proud parents stopped in to show him off. They were on the way over to the public health hospital to "pound" the child on the scale, and incidentally to borrow some reading matter. He was "very interesting" to read books with cartoons! I think my mother is a born linguist, for after I'd written home a few William-ism's, she answered, "I've just finished a bowl of popcorn, and am feeling very indigestible!"

* * *

Now let's read Chinese-English letters from friends, not to make fun of them, but to share the novel and very satisfactory way they expressed themselves. They are not just entertaining, but deeply significant to the thoughtful reader.

Here is a desperate appeal from a lad whose education we'd been helping to finance:

"My dear Mrs. Ma

"Before I have not written it, I want to thank you for your helpful me.

"Yesterday I'm going to ya priest home to meeting him. He said, About my expense of school that he didn't know, and he said. Because Mrs. Ma have not letter to give him. Therefore he didn't know. I explain for him during the time. I said Mrs. Ma who helped me that was all my other expense. About my expense of school that was from an the meeting to helping me. But he still not know, I'm very despair, I have not studing from now on. What should be done from now on? pleasing you help me. I shall remember it to my dying day. pleasing you back letter to me. pleasing you correct for me the letter.

> "Bless you
> "New Year happy
> "Student Wang"

A professional report concerning who had been using an endowed hospital bed:

"A cloudy day in May, 1948. A typhoid patient was transported to social service department and asked for medical succor. He was a middle-aged man, named Tuan Sze Chang. Who ignorant was. Trade occupied his whole life, but he did not obtain much profit to support his family, because he had no enough capital.

"He lived with his wife and three children and always struggled against hunger and cold. The elder son already arrived at the age of education and still played at home. How sorrowful his father was. Just that time. The miserable evil was caming to that family, the father infected tyephoid because he did not take care of his health in the effected of over work.

"At first, he wanted to save money and did not go to hospital to see the docter. He endured the pain until he was in a critical state. During the diagnosis, the docters found that his intestines was breaking and much blood flowing out. So he was brought to one sick room by SSD's helping and begun to mend the intestines with operation by docters. But in vain he died after two days and wasted 13,845,000 dollers for medicine, special food, laboratory, dressings, operation and rent his family did not pay."

A university student in the north writes a touching Christmas letter:

"Dear Mr. M.,

"I did not write you for a long time. This year will soon be ended and Christmas will draw nigh. I hope that you will have a very Merry Christmas. Because we are in a National University that we shall not have a holiday on Christmas, but I will try to have a good time when that day. Perhaps we would have snow on that day, which will make this great day happier.

"We are on a long strike in which 17 days had already gone, and none can tell when shall the strike go to an end. The cause of this strike is that we have no president for more than a year, and the University has no enough money. The students are in a very sad situation, and nobody would take care of them. They have no enough dormitories, no good apparatus in laboratory, and no enough books in library. The library is just being built. But for the shortage of money and the weather is so cold that cement freezes immediately, after it is mixed with water, it is stopped now. The present library is the poorest one in all the universities, I think, because it occupies only a small room.

"Even fighting is very near to Tientsin (less than 20 miles from the city) it seems to us nothing more suffering than the prices and the cold weather. The terrific inflation had made us very difficult fee for board goes up and up every fortnight and the food becomes worse and worse. A bag of flour costs $700,000 today and $30,000 a pound of meat. And it is still going up and up. Everyone knows what will the result be but none can give a plan to avoid it!

"It is said that the minimum temperature here is -20° C., and now it is about -14° C. Water keeps freezing and it had snowed very heavily a few days before. It's a kind of torture to write something in such cold weather, even though there is a furnace in our room.

"After having lived in university for nearly three months, I found that it is very dry and monotonous in studying engineering, and its troublesome and tiring to do counting all the day. I should study English literature or pure science as Physics or chemistry because I am interesting in them. The reason I did not choose one from these here is that I thought China does not need English literature so eagerly as she needs engineers. I thought I could not get enough knowledge if I study chemistry or physics because there are no good and new apparatus and books in Chinese universities, even though there are many learned professors. And many students found themselves unemployed as soon as they graduated. I am afraid that I shall be in the same condition, if I study English Literature or Pure Science. I hope you will tell me your opinion about this problem. Because not only I, but also Jim, Harold, and thousands of the Chinese students have the same trouble.

"I am now reading, and I will use the time in the nearly infinite strike for my English because my English is really gone back, and I had got a very little time to read English books before this strike, and I could hardly get a good English book.

"Strikes seem to come in continuity. Someone in T. initiated a strike for 'Anti-Starvation' and I predict that this strike will spread all over the country if the government does not appreciate it.

"Yours sincerely,"

❀   ❀   ❀

Because of a slight eye operation, I was late in moving from Chengtu to Hochwan. Don came to the Chungking airport to meet me, and while waiting made friends with Henry, a young Christian who was the radio operator. After that Henry was kind and helpful, often sending us English papers which came in on the planes. Here follows a delightful series of notes which came with the papers:

"Dear Mr. McCammon,

"Thank our father help me to got chance to met you and your wife down the airport that day, and I was so glad to be able to became one of your friends—and hope you would tell me many many wonderful things about our god later on.

"Through miss N. I learned that you have been arrived Hochwan ready. How are you and yours getting on right now? There will be no more trouble about her eye now?

"Attach here with Shanghai paper it just came in with the ship this afternoon hope it would be possible to kill your couple hours. God bless you and yours to be happy and healthy.   "I'm

"Sincerely yours,
"Henry"

"Dear Don,

"We were so glad to read your letter of the 3th inst. and I am sorry to say that I was so lazy did not wrote any word to you in the past weeks and beg you apology on that.

"Have you get the radio from state? We understant it is very bad for you to stay in the rough country and cut off all of the news from outside. I was unable to sent you any papers for the past as you know the flights all cancelled for the past weeks due to the refueling airport on the way from Shanghai to Chungking were under construction. Though there were couple ships in for special, most of it were service for cargo.

"The attached papers were came from one of the company fellow, so it had been delayed for days, I suppose it would be still new for you. I will try my best to be able to get chance to have the paper for you on occasion. This noon we have one ship in from Hunkong, but I was disopointed to found out there were no English paper on board at all.

"We were sorry to learned that your building is still under going, and the financial dificulty, and the workers made many troubles for you. We Bless God may you to find out one honest man or two to finish the rest of the job.

"For your information Yeumee is expected to has a baby in the middle of the coming June, and we all gratefully to carry on our burden in the near future. By the way, may I know does your wife carry young already? We hope your both would be parenthood in the very near future.

"It would be very appreciated if you could correct any mistakes in this letter as you know I am not so hot in English.

"Yeumee sends her best wishes to you and your wife, and hope your both can be our gests in the near future.

"Your brother in the Lord,
"Henry"

"Dear Don,

"Did you receive to papers dated 5th instant? here is the papers of yeasterday's from Shanghai. I hope there would be many news for you and your wife to read and discuss for couple hours.

"By the way it makes me to ask you for the following transation as I received a letter from my close friend Mr. Young from Hankow today hunting for job. Mr. Young, a Christian, a very honest man, formerly he was working in Shanghai, meanwhile I was working in the same place. He was resigned from the Air Force for three months ago as he was ordered to be transferred out to Formosa which is so expensive place and impossible for him to suppose his parents with his poor salary. He is single man, 30 year old, with no any bad habites. so I think he would be the man be able to help you and the Church if you need to have one.

"The above transation I just like to let you know there is a man, and if necessary for you in your end, but I am not quite sure which they are possible to be here or no, as there is a distance from Hankow to Chungking. I had been arranged one of my room for his parents in Chungking, which was originally I asked him to have his parents here when the siduation was bad in Shanghai for evacuation. I will try my best to have them here if there is need in your end.

"Best wiches for you and your wife.

"Your brother in The Lord
"Henry"

Finally, I will trust you with three sweet notes from Nurse Julia. If anyone laughs at these he's no longer my friend!

This came after she heard that Don had been deported:

"Your letter came last night. It almost broke my heart. I cried and cried. I am sorry for you. I only wish I could hold your hand and let us cry together and pray together too. I went down to the prayer room to bend the knee in prayer until the midnight. I slept and dreamed and cried. When the tear go out. I woke and saw the night still dark. I got up and went to the prayer room again. At there God comforted me. Gave me His real peace. I believe all things were God's well. Because Rom. 8:28. I think I should write a letter to your mother (also is mine!) and tell her my address. She can send me a telegram when D. is get there. Then I can telegraph to you. I do pray especially for him. God shall care him. May this short letter bring my warm heart and all of my love."

She sent me a Chinese hymnbook for my birthday, with this note:

"I pray that when you play with it and your heart will fill full of happy and thankful and comfortable from God."

Do you wonder that I loved to get her letters?

This precious bit was written on a Christmas card which we miraculously received after I was back in the States. Not only did it bring reassuring news of Julia, but in one sentence she told us that B., an old Hochwan helper, is standing strong in the Lord. He had strayed far the last we knew, in his zeal to serve his country.

"I am so happy for you have Christmas in home. May we have a special prayer on that day. I miss you so much, but in prayer I feel so tung [close] with you! I am busy and happy and have good health too. God leads me in every way. I have entered the church which I liked best and every week take holy communion at there. B. is like the prodigal son. I specially thank the Lord for him. it is so wonderful! his witness helped seven people repented on a preaching meeting. he prayed almost with all the night and all of us prayed hard too. We saw God's glory. Ps. 27:4 is my life. Ps. 16 is too. You know how very love you I am."

I was very love her, too!

12. Pig Home Street

A much-used phrase in the Chinese language is to "eat bitterness." Most of them eat it, daily, with no choice on their part. However, when they see someone voluntarily eat it, their admiration knows no bounds. The stories we heard about great foreigners they had known always idealized not so much those who had given things to the Chinese, but those who had *given up* comforts themselves.

So it was that Ruth's experiment in Chinese living made a real impression on her neighbors, and opened a door for evangelism which otherwise would have remained closed.

The evangelist helped her find, on the other side of town, a tiny house on Pig Home Street. "Pig" was a family name, but perhaps this street was so called because each night during the night meat was slaughtered there for the next day's market. Actually any street was pig home street, for pigs in China live right with the family. It was nothing unusual, during a visit, to have a pig come grunting under the bench one was seated on, or during a meal to feel a pig rooting under the table!

Ruth took almost nothing with her—a cot, a tiny clay stove, a soon-blackened cooking pan, a table, some benches for guests, a washbasin, and a crock. She cooked just as her neighbors did, and ate what they could afford to eat. We kidded her about her vegetarian diet; we thought she was proving to the natives that foreigners don't really eat people! But truly she was proving something much more important than that. She was convincing them that she cared enough about knowing how their lot felt to sample it herself. And that was a language they understood.

It wasn't long until she had friends all along the way. Any time we went there we found her house full of playing children and idle women, asking, asking, singing, visiting. Soon we began weekly evangelistic meetings there; the adults crowded into her front room and the children met in a yard near by. I helped with the children, and their behavior, their singing, their understanding and recall of the stories was simply remarkable in contrast to meetings we had held in other areas. The difference lay in Ruth's presence during the week, and the convincing testimony she was living among them.

Several adults and children came to Sunday morning worship service and other meetings at our church clear across the town, and a number of them became Christians. Ruth moved back home in three months, for the intense heat was soon coming, but I am sure the neighbors are still talking about Miss Bi and the bitterness she ate voluntarily!

* * *

We always felt sorry not to be able to send resident workers to our outstations, for they were in great need of encouragement and leadership. Occasional visits could assure them of our continued concern for their welfare, but until we had more co-workers, both Chinese and foreign, we could do little more. You have read already about the encouraging group we found in "12-Hole-Bridge." We were saddened at our last reports from there. They were a well-to-do group, on the whole, and one which would suffer at the hands of the Communist leveling process. Before the "liberators" came we heard that in this town everyone was carrying a gun and they were determined to fight to hold their property. Afterwards visitors from there told us of various leaders who had been killed and others who were in prison.

To balance this bad news, however, we saw a wonderful and humbling manifestation of God's power in another place.

Our closest outstation, Cloud Gate Place, had been on the completely dead list in our mental files. Then a group of convalescing Nationalist soldiers were sent there to live. Among them were a number of genuine Christians. They asked whether they might use the church building for meetings and eventually two of them lived in the property. Before we took over the responsibility, the former tenants had been forced out by a ruling that no one dealing in opium or prostitution was qualified to live there; so the place was empty. In the coming days it would have been impossible to hold empty buildings; so we were glad enough to have these two young men move in. They were uneducated, and their expression of their Christian experience was more emotional than ours, but God was using them. In the weeks and months when we could not visit them at all and our evangelist could go very seldom, the church thrived and developed. Before we left China our evangelist and his wife spent a week with this Cloud Gate Place Church, and having satisfied himself as to the soundness of the believers' faith and understanding, John administered the rite of baptism to sixteen candidates.

One very helpful practice which the wounded soldiers introduced to the local group was the singing of Psalms. It made memorization much easier for the people who couldn't read, and helped literate and illiterate alike to hide God's Word in their hearts against a coming day when they couldn't freely use their Bibles. At first the Chinese tunes sounded impossible, and we wondered how they could possibly remember what phrase came next, but soon we found ourselves singing along with them, everyone in unison as always in Chinese music, few "fa's" and "ti's," for the Chinese don't do well with half steps, and no raised eyebrows if the biggest man there suddenly sailed off above our heads in complete falsetto —that was a common occurrence.

✿　✿　✿

Hit-Iron Street was another regular preaching point in Hochwan, and this area remained open to us longer than any other. Even at the end, when we ourselves felt sure that for their sakes we must no longer go there, some of the simple old ladies would still ask, "Why don't you come any more? It was lots more fun when you came!" Christine was always a favorite with the folks on this street, and they with her too; so I'll let her tell it:

"'Sing song has come,' or 'hear Jesus,' are the words of welcome we hear as we turn the corner and start down Hit Iron Street every Wednesday evening at dusk. As we walk down the street, the children come to follow Dorothy and Julia, our Chinese nurse, who have charge of the children's meeting. By the time they reach the home where the meeting is held, there is a sticky little hand holding onto each of their ten fingers, and many more children following behind— dirty children, undernourished children, children with skin diseases. But they all have happy faces. They are eager to sing the songs, hear the Bible stories, and best of all, receive a picture card. These children do not have nice shiny red chairs to sit on. Some of them bring their own tiny benches, but many of them stand. Being normal children, they are often naughty or inattentive, but it is amazing how well they know the story and memory verse at the end of the hour.

"While the children are gathering together, the adults, too, are busy folding up tables and arranging benches in an open teashop. The owner of the teashop is not a Christian, but is, as the Chinese say, 'much polite,' and he seems to receive a great deal of pleasure from inviting us to his home.

"While the teashop furniture is being arranged, several of us start down the street to remind the adults that it is Wednesday evening. They need the reminder, for most of them keep no track of the day of the week or the hour of the day. Hit Iron Street is a street of very poorly constructed matchbox-like shops made of bamboo and a few boards. The men here all 'hit iron,' or are blacksmiths. They, with their families, have their homes in their shops. Sometimes even two or three families live in one shop. The Chinese people work from dawn until dusk, and as we start down the street, the shop fronts have just been boarded up, except for one board left open to serve as a door. As we come to the open door, the family is usually seated around the table eating the evening meal of rice and one vegetable. Their supper has been cooked over the same fire that has served their forge during their working hours. The room is dimly lighted by one small vegetable-oil lamp, or maybe just the light of the fire. As we say, 'Come, hear the Gospel tonight,' they look up, and most of them say, 'As soon as we have finished supper we will come.'

"It takes a half hour or sometimes an hour before the tea-shop is filled with people, for the Chinese are no respecters of time. The first part of our meeting is singing, and, although few of them read and some can't carry a tune, they love to sing simple choruses.

"The Chinese even have trouble with their own language! One evening Gordon, our Chinese pastor, was teaching them a song, 'Peace and joy, peace and joy, who believes on Jesus will receive salvation!' Later in the evening one woman asked, 'Is it really true that if we believe on Jesus we can sleep well at night?' The mistake was easily understood, for the difference in meaning is expressed only in tone, and the tones are lost in singing.

"Hit Iron Street is not like our modern American congregations. If Gordon does not preach long enough, they won't go home and he has to preach again! Once the meeting is ended, they linger to ask questions—very simple questions— you can't even realize how simple unless you've lived in the Orient. 'Can you pray any time or any place?' asked one woman. A man said, 'My little girl believes. You know, it's easy for her to believe. My trouble is that I have not yet repented. I still smoke!' One woman asked, 'My baby has diarrhea. Will you pray for him?' I said I would pray for the child, but also suggested that she bring him to our clinic the next morning. She said, 'Oh, I don't have time to bring him to the clinic, and I forget to pray, but I want you to pray for him. Will you?' Another woman remarked to her friend, 'My, this religion is much less trouble than ours. We need to go to the temple all the time to burn incense and pay the priest money!'

"When our farewells have been said and all the polite Chinese bows have been made, we take our leave. But they still accompany us to the end of the street, for it is a good Chinese custom to 'send' guests. As we leave, they say, 'Can't you come twice a week? We hear one time and then we go our way and forget again.'

"We covet these people so much for the Lord that we sometimes become impatient because results are not greater. But we take heart anew when we remind ourselves that only a few months ago they had never even heard the name of Jesus."

13. "Stir - Fry" Style

We went to China grimly determined to like her and her ways. Our grim determination was extremely unnecessary, for the Chinese are a lovable people.

One phase of Chinese life which is especially pleasant to adapt to is the food—we really loved it and often get hungry for it since we're home from China. At first we remembered too many "birds' nest" stories from childhood days, and were highly suspicious of everything we ate. Also, we had been unduly frightened by well-meant warnings from experienced missionaries who knew that one must actually build up his bodily resistance. It is a fact that the Chinese ate certain cold dishes, for instance, which had never been scalded, and which at first might have upset us. Later on we struck a happy balance between fear and common sense, and enjoyed life much more.

Soon after we arrived in China we attended a feast. My letter home describing it reflects my immature and unwarranted suspicion of everything that didn't look just like Indiana ham and eggs!

"One of our language school friends gave a feast recently; I'll try to remember most of the things we ate. She had asked a Chinese friend to go along, to help in ordering food and in being host, since she didn't know all the customs any more than we do. This boy found a very nice restaurant. We had a white tablecloth, paper napkins, and cold boiled water to drink with our meal, three very foreign features for a true Chinese meal. When we came in we were seated at one long table, and served tea and salted watermelon seeds. For the first time I found myself getting along nicely with cracking the seeds between my teeth and extracting the tiny kernel without either looking or touching. Try it sometime. Then the food was ready, and we moved to the usual, round table. The guests of honor are seated the farthest from the serving door, and on down the list till the host is nearest the door. The first thing our host did was to take his napkin and clean his chopsticks, bowl, and little condiment dish. We followed his example, although I fear rubbing with a napkin doesn't take many germs off. When we go out to eat, we always ask for boiling water to dip our dishes in, but when one is a guest, he doesn't make so bold. The first dish was a cold plate, with several types of cold meat loaf, all in tiny pieces of course, some chicken gizzard, whole little fish, and shrimp, complete from head to toe. In the middle of the platter were century eggs, eggs which have been left in lime for a long, long time, until the yolk has become dark and the white gelatinous. I ate my first century egg, and it wasn't so bad, if you refer only to taste and not appearance.

"The next dish scared me most. It was a thick, stew-ish sort of concoction, but everything that was pulled out seemed to me at least semi-questionable. There was stomach, and when Luella asked 'whose?' none of our Chinese friends answered. There was eel-skin, and windpipe, intestine and kidneys. I personally downed—after five minutes of contemplation—something that looked exactly like what we've been chasing in our bedroom and putting DDT down for; legs all over the thing! [I later learned that it was merely a fancy-cut piece of kidney.] After that things got progressively better. An egg roll, stuffed with meat—delicious. A plate of sweet-sour pork, which is item number one every time we go out to eat Chinese food. A huge fish perfectly done with just a bit of *la*—Szechwan red pepper. A couple of beautiful plates of steamed bread, heavy, damp, and tasteless. The sweet dish of the meal was a junket floating in syrup; not very sweet—just slightly flavored with the seeds of some fruit we didn't recognize. There must have been a few more dishes, since the sweet dish usually comes about the middle of the meal. Anyway, our last dish, as always, was soup, and it was the most delicious soup I have ever eaten. First we devastated the whole duck which was in the middle of the bowl, and then we filled our bowls with soup and drank from them. It was the first feast I'd attended where we didn't eat rice or noodles at all; they offered them to us, but none of us had any room! When we'd moved back to the other table, visited a bit more, had some more tea, and cracked some more melon seeds, our host and hostess called rickshas for us, paid our fare home, and the party was over."

When one goes to a Chinese restaurant in the States, he usually has Cantonese food, which is quite different from Szechwanese. Szechwanese is freely flavored with red pepper, and just can't be improved on, we think. There are actually two flavors used a lot, *la jyiao*, or red pepper, *hwa jyiao*, a completely effective anesthetic which renders the whole mouth and throat numb, and a ground up version of *hai jyiao*—which Olin aptly describes as making the food taste as though a dirty dishrag had been dragged through it. We stick to *la* only, but in strength enough to surprise and please the Chinese.

"Did you eat with chopsticks?" many friends ask. Indeed we did. We learned quickly on our trip inland from Shanghai, for it was the only way to get the food! We never became so adept as a boy I heard of who caught flies with chopsticks, but we acquired facility enough to look after ourselves very satisfactorily at a Chinese meal. What was more difficult for us to learn was the Chinese courtesy which goes with a feast. It took all the patience we had (and sometimes more) to hesitate, wait, argue, and defer in the matter of who should enter the room first when we were called. Christine's prematurely gray hair often settled this a bit more quickly. Once there, we did the same polite objecting to being given seats at the table—surely we should all have lower seats! And finally, in our famished conditions (because feasts are never on time) we had to sit back a few minutes more, contemplating the tempting, sizzling dishes, waiting for someone else to help himself first. Eventually the host would break the deadlock by reaching a few guests a morsel with his chopsticks, after which everyone reached toward the dish, still holding back until the host said "please, please, please." The most polite (or the most controlled) got there just a bit later than the others.

Feast tables are round, and passing of the food unnecessary. Everyone helps himself from the main dishes, and each has his own rice bowl, teacup, and condiment dish. The host thoughtfully rearranges the dishes as more are added so that everyone has a chance to reach all of them. There are supposed to be about as many main dishes as there are guests, with a soup or two extra and the rice (or noodles) not counted in. At elaborate feasts, however, the count may well go to two main dishes per guest. We often regretted our early intemperance when the last dishes found us utterly stuffed, but one never knew for sure how to allocate his capacity. When eating Chinese food a shy creature will only pick a few bites from the dishes nearest him, but someone who feels hungry and at home may stand up and reach halfway across the table to get something which appeals to him. A few more modern hosts or those who had studied abroad sometimes tried (for our sakes, mostly) to arrange separate serving chopsticks and soup serving spoons but usually everybody got mixed up and soon the "public" utensils were confused with the "private" ones. That never bothered me unless we had an extra fussy guest who was never satisfied with what he brought out of the bowl the first time, and would drop it back to hunt for something more to his liking.

The Chinese are taught never to take food in their hands;

8

so a bony piece goes into the mouth and the bones are spat onto the table. For this reason the table is bare and washable, and the hands remain clean and dry for effective chopstick maneuvers. An occasional small bone is just as easily spat on the floor. At the end of the meal, small cups of warm water are often served for the specific purpose of rinsing the mouth. After a few "squooshes" like an after-toothbrush-rinse the water is spat over one's shoulder onto the dirt floor. A refreshing but doubtless unsanitary custom is the passing of wet towels for a quick cleanup after a meal. At an elaborate feast there are individual towels, wrung out of very hot perfume-scented water, but at a less formal affair several people may use the same towel, and sweaty men may wash their entire shaven heads with it before passing it on. Eye diseases are easily spread in this way, and it was not unusual to see posters from the health department displayed in public eating houses, discouraging this practice.

The hostess who wishes to honor her guest goes into the kitchen and prepares the meal herself, though she may ordinarily have a full-time cook. She may not appear at the feast at all, or perhaps just long enough to deprecate her wonderful meal. The less traditional hostess may want to enjoy the meal with her guests, in which case they go to a good restaurant where the food has been carefully ordered ahead of time, or a cook and the food may be brought to the home from such a place.

Meals vary tremendously in China. I wonder if there have ever been two whole meals which were exact duplicates. It was a rare experience even to find two dishes which were identical. The more meat in the meal, the fancier it was considered, with fish, other sea foods, and chicken or duck rating as chief luxuries. Meat, in our section, meant pork, pork, pork, and a difficult adjustment for our stomachs to face was the fact that fat pork was a special delicacy. In fact, sometimes it wasn't even fat pork, but just plain pork fat, and it felt as though it would come up considerably easier than it had gone down!

We knew it was true, but never got used to the fact that a previous engagement or even having already eaten was no excuse for not going to a feast on a last-minute invitation. One could go late, leave early, and eat almost nothing, but unless he appeared he was offending his host. I remember one meal we appreciated a great deal in spite of the unexpected summons which came just after our own dinner was finished. It was in meaningful contrast to many feasts we had attended.

This poor family lived on White Flower Street, a street where only coal was sold. The husband worked on a coal-hauling boat and was seldom home. Both of them came to church when they could. On this day the husband was home; so they came inviting us to dinner. The meal was ready, there was no refusing; so we went.

Their bedroom, living room, and kitchen were all one room, facing out onto the street. We foreigners created a great sensation, and immediately the entire street side of the room was lined with observers. The small square table was pushed up to the edge of the hard bamboo bed, for there weren't benches enough for all sides. There was only one dish other than the rice, but a very plentiful supply of it bubbled in the pot there beside us. It was a vegetable stew predominated by mushy Chinese potatoes and flavored by a tiny bit of pork. The food was delicious and the fellowship was warm. We went home satisfied in mind and body, happy that those friends had been content to share what they had, rather than spend a lot on luxuries they could ill afford.

A still more unique approach to a meal was related by Christine and Luella after a visit with the evangelist to "12-Hole-Bridge." It was Sunday morning, and the three of them went to the church expecting to conduct morning worship. After quite a long wait they were approached by a silk-gowned gentleman, a member of the congregation, who invited them to take a walk. They protested that they expected to have church, but he assured them that nobody would come for a while. He led them through the country to his home. After a long wait with a cup of tea, they saw a servant come in from gathering eggs and soon they were served hard boiled eggs. Another long silent interval, then a servant came through on his way from the cornfield. Soon hot roasting ears were passed. Along in the middle of the afternoon the host appeared to bid them to dinner and a marvelous meal followed. The people at "12-Hole-Bridge" were acquainted with the foreigners' favorite foods, and always served them all. A unanimous favorite with our group was their "lambs' tails," bits of dough fried in deep fat and liberally sprinkled with sugar. Eventually Gordon suggested again that they should go to church, but the host said the people wouldn't be there yet. Then leisurely tea, and a tour of the estate, after which the host said he would take them back in his boat. They had a picturesque cruise past the rice fields, arriving at the church just as the first worshipers came down the path. Soon the group had gathered and they held services as they had planned to do some seven hours earlier. The host knew Gordon well enough to realize that he wouldn't want to postpone church just for a feast; so never did tell him what was going to happen next!

It was on this same trip that poor Gordon was an unwilling martyr. One concoction which some Chinese relish, but which we found totally impossible, is called *dan wher*. It is warm, slightly fermented rice wine, with a raw egg whipped into it. When guests call to see a new baby, the wine is served with a whole poached egg, which is drinkable. But early in the morning on the day they started home, neither Christine nor Luella could face this brew. Obliging Gordon gulped it down for them when their hostess was out of the room, but confided on the way home that he detested it too!

Noodles and other flour products are really North China foods, and Szechwan is purely a rice district. There were noodle shops, though, in Hochwan, and some of us often got hungry for a noodle meal. Their noodles are very fine, just paste with no eggs, and even a moment's overcooking made a sticky mess. That never happened to the Chinese, but we had some learning to do before we could fix them at home. We'd prepare the rice bowl with a touch of *la*, a dash of soy sauce, a taste of vinegar, then into the boiling water went the noodles, and just before they came out again they were joined by a sprig of pea vine tip or some other quick-cooking green. Now quickly into the prepared bowl, stir the mixture through them, and "slurrp—ready for another bowl!" At the portable noodle stands along the street one could get an endless variety of noodle flavors. Some were from meat stocks, such as chicken, fish, pork; some were from dried herbs, dried sea food, or mushrooms; some featured fresh vegetables, and some flavorings came out of mysterious little bottles of powder whose English equivalent we never did discover. Cold noodles in the summertime were really a trick to manage. They had to be cooled without getting sticky. They were liberally sprinkled with red pepper and eaten about like a salad. Almost too hot a food to cool one off, but we liked them very much.

Another northern food was *jyiao-dz*. We never learned to make these; it took Mrs. Thunder and a couple of helpers simply hours; so we thought it might take us days. They were small pastry-covered balls of meat and vegetable, preferably steamed but boiled would do. We dipped them in vinegar, red pepper, and soy sauce and I could sometimes consume thirty at one meal.

Before Mrs. Thunder left, Christine learned all she could from her about cooking Chinese food. Just as any cook has her own little touches which she finds difficult to explain or is unwilling to divulge, so a Chinese cook never seemed quite able to tell it all. But Christine learned to cook Chinese food which we all enjoyed, then taught Ruth and me enough to cook an occasional edible meal.

I see by a Chinese cookbook that what we made most often was called a "stir-fry" dish. This book, by the way, is Christine's favorite on Chinese foods: *How to Cook and Eat in Chinese* by Buwei Yang Chao, published by the John Day Company, New York.

We chopped our pork in tiny bite size cubes, mixed in bean starch (cornstarch in this country) and soy sauce, till it was sticky and the starch was all wet. Then we fried it quickly in lots of grease (the Chinese use still more) on a hot fire. If the vegetable we were adding was tender and leafy, we just stirred bits of it through the cooked pork till they were hot and served it. If it was a more stalky vegetable inclined to need cooking, we sometimes added a bit of water and covered the pan a few minutes, being careful not to overcook it. The trick of "stir-fry" dishes is to have things chopped finely enough so that one glance at the hot frying pan cooks them. The preparation takes time; cooking is done in the twinkling of an eye.

Chinese cooks don't use pan after pan. Their sole pan is built right into their stove. The rounded-bottom of this iron "go" sits down in the fire; so it takes only a few twigs to cook a dish. As soon as it is served another is tossed in, and so it goes. The Indians cook rice in a lot of water, I understand. The Chinese use just enough so that the water is gone when the rice is done. The finished product tastes the same with both methods, and the busy American cook is usually safer and happier using more water.

Christine has selected these four recipes which she has used in this country, and which most Americans enjoy. They are all things we ate and liked in China, yet nothing one needs to "get used to" before appreciating. Try them!

EIGHT PRECIOUS PUDDING

1 lb. glutinous rice (regular rice may be used)
½ cup sugar

Various available candied fruits and nuts, ideally totaling eight. Candied lotus seeds, almonds, walnuts, fresh peanuts, seedless raisins, candied cherries, candied citron, or what have you—all in small quantities.

Simmer the rice in 2 cups of water until rice is slightly soft. Add the sugar and another cup of water and simmer for 15 minutes more.

On the bottom of a large bowl, arrange the fruits and nuts in some attractive design. Carefully pour the drained rice onto the fruits. Rest the bowl on a stand in water and steam for three hours in a covered pot. Turn out on a platter and serve with a tart lemon sauce. (Our cook added a little lard to the rice and sugar to the fruit.)

Egg Flower Soup

1 qt. chicken broth
½ cup finely chopped water chestnuts
2 eggs
salt and pepper

Pour water chestnuts into the boiling broth. Cook for about five minutes. Pour beaten eggs into the boiling broth and stir slowly but well until eggs form small "flowers." Add salt and pepper to taste.

Sweet Sour Pork (serves 3)

½-¾ lb. pork, chopped in pieces 1" x 2" x 4"
½-¾ cup pineapple
1 large green pepper cut in wedges
4 heaping T. brown sugar
2 T. pork or bacon fat
6 T. dark Karo
5 T. vinegar (varies with strength of vinegar)
3 T. soy sauce
1 t. ginger
3 T. cornstarch

Caramelize brown sugar, add pork fat immediately; when two are mixed as much as possible, add Karo. Then add vinegar, soy sauce, and ginger. Cook until lumps are smoothed out.

Mix cornstarch with pineapple juice to make a thin, smooth sauce. Stir enough into above mixture to make a heavy syrupy sauce. Add pepper wedges, pineapple, and last the cooked pork.

To prepare the pork, roll it in cornstarch and fry quickly in drippings until brown.

After adding the pork to the mixture, leave mixture on the fire only long enough to heat through—not more than five minutes. If mixture gets too thick, add more pineapple juice.

CHICKEN AND WALNUTS

1 young chicken
$\frac{1}{2}$ lb. walnut or almond meats
$\frac{1}{8}$ lb. water chestnuts
10 large-sized black mushrooms (or whatever mushrooms are available)

Fry nut meats until slightly brown and crisp. Remove meat of raw chicken from bones, cut into small cubes, and fry in a hot pan with a little fat.

Soak mushrooms in warm water and cut into cubes.

Blanch water chestnuts and cut into cubes, then fry mushrooms and chestnuts in the same manner as the chicken.

Add mushrooms and chestnuts to chicken with a small piece of ginger chopped fine, a dash of soy sauce, and salt and pepper to taste.

To this mixture add browned nut meats, stirring whole thing well. Serve hot.

14. Come the "Liberators"

Closer, closer, closer came the Communist armies. For years, months, and weeks we had been hearing and reading and writing rumors about the coming turnover. In the last days before the "liberators" arrived at Hochwan, and in the first months of the occupation, I kept a "liberation diary." This and the following chapter are excerpts from that diary.

Nov. 30, 1949: The radio says Chungking (60 miles away) is in the process of turnover. The Nationalist Government has gone to Chengtu; no communication with Chungking. People here fleeing to the country. All full of fear, grabbing what they can carry in two hands. A really tragic drama passing our gate from dawn until dark.

Dec. 2: Peipei (halfway to Chungking from here) said to have fallen last night. Retreating troops passing all morning. We prepare for the eventuality of fire. What to take! Packing sleeping equipment and warmest woolens. It was mostly a process of deciding *against* various items. The things of this world have pretty definitely lost their glamour. Two possibilities we face—the looters who may come between the retreat and the occupation, or burning of the city by the retreating army. We consider sitting up in shifts tonight, but at the moment we're all too sleepy.

Liu Ma (the old lady who lives in the parsonage and cooks for the boys) still trying desperately to get to her son in Chungking, but no boats will take her. She weeps day and night. Already spent a foolish, foodless, sleepless two days and two nights trying to get to Peipei in a tiny wooden boat, but she had to return. Gordon, our evangelist, comes back from two days at the first station north. He was the only passenger on the only boat. Everyone going the other way. Saw people, people, all day long, leaving the city. They can't get carriers; so even the old ladies and little children carry big packs on their backs. At evening it was finally deathly quiet. Put our silver dollars in a gunny sack to throw down the cistern if we had to leave.

Had special afternoon coffee just for fun. I made apple butter coffee cake and we ate the Swiss cheese E. brought us from Hong Kong. Our password, "We must go into this thing well nourished," as we devour everything special we've been saving. I really think we're nervous—I'm sure it isn't hunger! Cinnamon drops and pineapple go today. Chocolate chips and coconut on the ticket for tomorrow. The town is virtually deserted. We should be "liberated" when we wake up in the morning, but after two years of imminency, it likely can be postponed a bit longer.

Dec. 3: Last night was a restless one. Quiet as death till midnight—the dogs didn't even bark. (At that point, my diary says, "Not even the dogs barked," but somehow that sounds queer!) Then shots in the street just outside woke us, but we never did find out where they came from. Don finally got up at 2:00 and stayed up. People still leaving town in the morning, and the continual sound of gunfire on the river front. About 11:00 A.M. everyone reappeared and rushed down the street to buy firecrackers and welcome the conquering Communists. They came in peacefully, covered with mud and dead tired. The Nationalists retreated just ahead of them— some of them had to run to get out of sight in time; so there was no period of disorder when local scalawags could loot. The shooting was not at anyone. It was just to get answers so that they would know where the oncomers were, and how soon to pull out.

The sun is out bright for the first time in days. Our era of restricted freedom is about to begin. The first report says 300 men came in and took over where 20,000 pulled out. There surely should have been no lives lost, but probably a few people were too careless. Evening: Don finds out firsthand that Americans are not loved by the Communists. One soldier with the red star on his cap suggested killing him, and others made unenthusiastic observations about his nationality. One gave out with the usual cheerful *ding how*, but Don admits he looked downright stupid!

We learned this P.M. that one of our church members, Mrs. Li, was killed by a piece of shrapnel from a Nationalist shell. Julia, our nurse, went and gave sulfa to another lady who was wounded in the same explosion, and a baby whose eye was put out. She can't do anything for their wounds—they must go to the Peipei hospital—but she can give preventives against infection. No doctor to be found except one who gave himself the title. He has a piece of shrapnel in his head from the last war and acts like it. Christine finds Matthew 10 in line for tomorrow's English Bible class: "If men persecute you in one town, flee to the next." And mine says, "Marvel not if the world hate you—we ought to lay down our lives for the brethren."

Dec. 4: English Bible attendance—zero, of course. Mr. Li comes to ask us to help bury his wife. The new soldiers bring People's Government money at $4,000 to $1 silver. Here we go again! Had a worship service with no sermon. A really heartening group came, and the spirit was good. Sunday school (formerly up to 250), one class for all the children—eight. Then over the river to a family worship service and the closing of Mrs. Li's casket. (You should see these caskets. Made of huge slabs of wood!) Five children, who were awfully pathetic. When Mr. Li introduced us to them, they bent down till their heads hit the floor, and came up bowing as though to idols. The whole service was conducted in the midst of 300 Communist soldiers who were "borrowing" the home and yard for a couple of days. They crowded around and looked and listened. Even read over our shoulders as we sang from the hymnal. Really, it took courage on the part of Mr. Li to invite us, just when a lot of our friends are scared to admit they know us. And this week he came and said he wished we could come once a week to have a home worship service to help teach his children and any of the neighbors who want to come. It is a real opening.

Dec. 5: Left the house at 6:30 A.M. to bury Mrs. Li. Notices on the street say the liberators intend to protect foreigners and that the people may believe whatever they like. We sat at Li's for hours till they finally served breakfast. The 300 soldiers had pulled out early and used the kitchen facilities first; so slowed down the family. Mr. Li said they were very careful and considerate, and returned everything they'd borrowed before they left. They don't resemble their predecessors in this point. The workmen came and while we looked on they daubed shut the casket. Then we all ate a bit of breakfast and had a service. Don went on to the country for the actual burial, but we girls begged off and came home frozen at 11:00. Don got home at 3:45. While we were waiting for breakfast, the chief mourner entertained us with stories of how the head of the city came to the bank where he works and ordered them to produce 3,000 hard silver dollars to pay the bribe the retreating soldiers asked to keep them from burning the city. This was impossible since their bank had been ordered by the same official not to deal in hard cash. Eventually they called in heads of the other banks, and among them scraped up $20,000 in paper. The soldiers could use that in the cities to which they were fleeing.

Strangely enough, there are no well-dressed people in town and none in foreign dress. A friend of ours who usually wears

G.I. khaki and combat boots, came back from the country today dressed in typical farmer pants and jacket, with mud carefully smeared on his new cheap cloth shoes. Says he, "I guess the liberating army wouldn't like me so well in the clothes I usually wear." I didn't even recognize a stylish lady I'd met a couple of times when she came this mornnig to tell us how their home was looted by retreating soldiers. No make-up, no jewels, no silk dress nor embroidered shoes. Just another country woman now.

Dec. 6: Patients in the clinic had no money yesterday; so Julia closed up shop. But today she is trying to make ways for them to pay, since the poor ones are the ones who need help the most, and they don't have silver to exchange for new money. The first customer paid with a pair of homemade scissors worth 1/10 of a deo of rice.

A friend comes to tell us about the lectures the liberators are giving. Three months and then cometh the change. Everyone will have an opportunity to go to school, all the way from kindergarten to college. Everyone will give four hours' work a day to the government, at whatever his profession. We will wear out the good clothes we have, but it is hoped that by the time they need replacements our thoughts will be changed and we will be convinced that local coarse clothing is good enough. (This is the people in general, not just the foreigners.) If we want luxuries, whether servants or fine possessions, we will pay a stiff luxury tax.

Late in the afternoon many troops came to town. One group put up for the night in all the homes along our street. A bunch of them burst into our yard and set down their stuff, but when I went out and they saw my foreign features, they said it was all a mistake, and bolted out. A young student friend of Ruth's came with a very concerned air, and placing his hand on her shoulder, whispered into her ear in his best English, "My dear, you must go home." Says he's heard something awful but won't say what!

Dec. 8: Principal C. calls to say that English Bible classes in the school are temporarily halted, but that if the new friends won't let him invite us back, he will "order" the pupils to church for the Sunday morning classes!

Dec. 10: Julie brings in the week's clinic money. Big old coppers from the old days, now worth one cent or two for one cent. Nickel money worth either 10 per cent or 20 per cent of the printed value, depending on the design on the border of it. Bills left from the silver regime, worth two cents on the dollar, and new People's money worth eleven cents silver to $400. An old lady from our church got home today after 18 days on a wooden boat from Chungking (60 miles). Tonight the street crier came banging down the street telling everyone to blow out the lights. There was a lone plane flying above—very unusual to hear a plane here—and they thought we were in for a bombing.

Dec. 18: Lots of soldiers on the streets these days and several visits from them. Wanted to borrow things, wanted to play ball on our court, wanted to try our keys to force open a neighbor's house to occupy it. So far we have got by with saying that it is not convenient, or just plain "no." I guess for non-resistants we are pretty resistant, but I'm afraid they'll be just like the camel in the tent once they get their noses in. Authentic word today of the awful massacre of the accumulation of political prisoners on the edge of Chungking. They were a Nationalist collection of several years—suspected Communists; so when things got hot, the Nationalists slaughtered them wholesale with knives, machine guns, and then fire. The "liberators" have left the whole spectacle untouched to show folks what the Nationalists were like. A few miraculously got out, and have told what it was like. Our nurse has word that twenty-some of her classmates have joined the new army. She is much taken by the thought of the bitterness they eat.

Jan. 1, 1950: The first of a three-day New Year's celebration proclaimed by the new government. Everybody marched and danced in the streets, with motivations ranging from fondness for the staff of life to their desire for a transcript. Everyone carried at least a small banner and many carried huge placards with striking illustrations. The Chinese are certainly artists—particularly when our country is involved. The whole noisy parade had to pass the church where we intended to have morning worship; so we stood outside and watched a good many.

Chengtu is finally reporting. They saw a lot more activity than we. There was much local trouble. One day the general in charge at the moment was losing his troops so rapidly that he ordered all city gates locked, and in a few hours had arrested more than a thousand men who had changed clothes!

Jan. 3: We are in Chungking on business, and hoping to go part way home by bus. Impossible to get to the boat early enough in the morning because of curfew. I don't know how the bus trip will proceed. Miss D. from the Methodist girls' school—about an hour out of town from here—told Don that their bus was stopped and everyone searched three times just in that hour's trip. The men had to strip down to their undershirts. Probably travel will become increasingly difficult from here on—that's one of the reasons we came when we did. In Hochwan it was easier than ever the day we came. The old water police were gone, of course, and nobody had succeeded them; so it was just a matter of walking onto the boat.

The future is a real unknown quantity. In a great many ways we are fortunate to be so noninstitutionalized. It is the schools and hospitals and other such institutions that are making the trouble just now. In our own tiny work, it has not been that we have any great convictions against institutions, but our minimum of personnel, both in full-time workers and in laymen, has of course not made it possible for us to have any institutional work yet. We need a church first, and church institutions afterward. And so our program has been clearly evangelistic from the day one. We hope and pray that always we will at least have the opportunity of individual and home contacts, which after all is a big area and awfully important to the foundational work which needs to be done.

15. More "Liberation Diary"

Jan. 24, 1950: What shall I say of the things that have happened here? Little things, by one's, but awfully big in total. Small things, in a big picture, but big ones in such a small frame as ours. School contacts all gone, of course. Orphanage likewise, and with a bad taste in the mouth. Our teacher, Sunday-school worker and a most dependable first fruit, gone. Not only gone but lied to us about it. She tried for officers' training school but flunked; so is in another school of indoctrination. No word yet except a few lines to her home. With her went a recent supposed convert—a boy, of whom we weren't very sure. Our second dependable and hopeful has tried her best to leave home, but her mother refuses permission. Number three Sunday-school teacher and about the only fragment left from the original flock as we found it has resigned because she soon will have to be going to work, and the two don't mix. P. is here and faithful, but wanting the worst way to leave. S. comes less frequently, and we are increasingly conscious of the fact that we know nothing about him.

James must go to Chengtu very soon for a delicate eye operation. Gordon plans to leave for school this summer. A prospective successor was here this week end, but neither he nor we thought it would work out. Don's instruction class of twelve is down to five. Young people everywhere are rushing off to join up. They have no money for tuition next term, nor do their families have money to support them at home. Some schools of 300-400 have less than 100 students left. The new program likes them young while it is easier to change their

9

ways of thinking. People in banks, schools, or government institutions of any kind are having a rough time on a few pounds of rice for themselves and no allowance for their dependents. Silver has become illegal in Chungking; still used here but will soon be out. In Chungking, schools were dismissed to send students out to encourage people to stop using silver. They are arrested for use, but will be released if they name three others who use it. There isn't enough JMP (people's government money) and silver can't yet be converted into it; so many people who have their funds in silver are dead broke, and have personal goods out on the street in hopes of a sale. Nobody buys anything. Our milkman is wasting gallons of precious milk; some can't buy and some don't dare.

Feb. 5: This week the pitch has changed a bit. Our near neighbors moved out and the new troops are girls. Most of them were in high school, or at that age, and so now any time we stop to listen we hear something that sounds like an enlarged version of a girls' dormitory, only the matron over there carries a whistle and a bugle. We are still enjoying our own quarters alone, but our friends at the China Inland Mission are entertaining 150 guests in their first and second floors. We are more and more thankful for our simple quarters; they don't look like much to the frequent housing committees who call to count the rooms. In fact, they are almost insultingly frank to say so! The town is full—a great many of them former students, and many more former defenders of the nation who have just changed their insignia. They are learning a big stock of new songs which are very catchy and attractive, but not all day every day.

Week before last we got a big brochure covering the items of information required for our first temporary registration. Don and the Chinese boys worked many hours writing up the answers, but when we four foreigners presented it at the government office, they found it *much* too brief for their purposes. We learned that although we thought their request hadn't been clear, it was really very clear indeed; so we gladly came home and spent more hours adding to various items—purposes, goals, history of ourselves and our church and our mission, church and personal property, etc. All of this is on file the better to protect us with, as promised in their Eight Points. The chap who interviewed us was very businesslike and reasonable. We found an English teacher friend and student of mine there to help with any language difficulties. It was a bit difficult to keep an expressionless face when he earnestly asked permission before offering one of us his pen to sign with. We are sure we understand better now what outsiders going into our land think of red tape. It isn't all there, be sure of that! The comrade's final tidbit was to tell us that since they have to protect us from all harm, they can do it better if we remain within the city limits, unless we have specific permission from him. And to get that permission, we need to have business which he considers important. He also stressed the fact that this was a *simple* registration, and that the actual giving of information would come later. What else there is to tell I haven't the faintest idea, but my guess is that we will do well to remember exactly, to the least detail, what we gave out with this time.

One day this week we thought the war of nerves had really started when we went out the gate and found four caskets lined up on our front sidewalk. Later it developed that they were just from the casket shop across the way, put over on our side so that the sun could shine on them. Some of our friends are a bit careful these days, especially in public, but the children on our streets still love us. They welcome us just as always, and the newcomers stand and stare in amazement! A few of the newly come girls have been brave (or foolish) enough to come in and visit with us.

Feb. 16: Tomorrow is New Year's Day, according to the Chinese calendar which everybody still goes by. Today the streets are full of people making last-minute purchases, and sending last-minute gifts. Everywhere it smells like cinnamon rolls; I think it must be the special flat white cakes of incense. Our own oven is full of drying sesame seed and I take it as an omen that our fate is sealed. Tomorrow morning at breakfast (of all meals) we will be confronted by the servants bearing dozens of sticky, perfume-flavored little white balls floating in sweet water, and we will each have to consume at least half a dozen to pass the test of courtesy. They are bad enough with meat, but worse with a sweet filling. Last night the servants were in the kitchen till late making a delicious sort of puffed rice and peanut candy. Did you know we had puffed rice? It's not shot from guns, but they dry it and then toss it on hot sand and it pops a little. Maybe Quaker wouldn't approve, but it's good for hot weather breakfast food. Earlier in the week, the cook and Mrs. Thunder, our woman helper, treated us to a marvelous New Year meal. She is a wonderful cook of Chinese food and had been preparing some items for weeks. For instance, the cold meats we ate first had been hanging in the yard on every sunny day since Christmas. Kidneys, bound tight in bamboo sticks on four sides so that when they are dried and sliced they look like four-leaf clovers. This year's pig ears had the black bristles removed, and we all enjoyed them. Last year that was the only item that stalled us. We had brains, done deliciously, and many other special treats which we genuinely enjoyed.

Things are bad in Szechwan. The farmers are afraid to venture on the road to town, the produce is less, and prices are up. Everyone is poor; not just the rich man. The landholders are poor, the poor are poorer, and the white-collar workers are hardest hit of all. Their income is less than that of Mrs. Thunder. The government knows it is a hard time for everyone, and tells them it has to be until Tibet is liberated and Formosa taken. Then everyone can settle down to not an easy life, but a less bitter one.

I have told you about our registration and the provision for our protection. We can no longer go out the city gate without written permission. Yesterday Ruth and Christine went to ask whether they might have permission to go to an outstation for several weeks or months. Our friend replied that there is no bureau in this city to issue such permits. I think the bureau will come, eventually, but it feels rather uncomfortable to know that there is no way to get permission to go anywhere, if we really needed it.

This week we have a delegation of students from the Chungking Seminary here to help with evangelistic work for several days. They're nice youngsters, but we are sobered again by seeing that it will be nigh onto impossible to find Chinese workers who agree with us in all the places we consider essential. If we agree here, we differ there. Training is the only answer, and that requires both teachers and students. It will be a long, long time before there can be a strong church in this city. The developments of the past weeks and months, coupled with the present conditions and the outlook for the future, make it pretty hard for us to be at all lighthearted. I don't think any of us has been as low in spirits as all of us are right at this moment. Although rights and freedoms and privileges are written down, yet all that our building program calls for involves young blood. And just now it is unusual to see anyone of the younger generation not in khaki. Our evangelistic program starts tomorrow, and goes for eight days. The CIM church and ours are co-operating. Mornings four groups will go out to four preaching places in the city. Afternoons, we have meetings for Christians, and evenings, a public evangelistic meeting in the church. Many shops are closed these days; so there is a chance for more people to come. Some are closed for the holidays, and some for other reasons. Unless the goods for sale are salt or rice or cheap vegetables, they have no business at all.

March 5: We have more new neighbors today. Last summer our next-door, just-over-the-wall neighbors almost completed a new two-story house. We were dreading the day they would move in, for they would almost be sitting in our laps. Before the turnover they just left the place empty and open. We never knew why the soldiers didn't take it. But last night in the night a new outfit came to town and did take it. Today they are noisily helping finish it; I think they must be putting floors in the upstairs. When I came out of our room this morning a lot of heads popped out of the upstairs windows to say "hello" and "good morning;" so I guess we are on good terms. Now Tinker, Don's dog, is standing in the yard barking in their direction, and a soldier is hanging out the window sawing on a Chinese fiddle. Oh, yes, the above remarks were in English, believe it or not, all but Tinker's!

March 13: It's a new age in China—people above the coolie class are learning to work. And some of them are even enjoying it. The boys in the church are undertaking a filthy project today, which formerly they couldn't and wouldn't have touched. Don is helping them. They dismantled the toilet building, picked up the pieces and moved them over, cleaned out the pit, stomped down the dirt, and are putting in a new lining. Several of them are right down in the slime, glorying in their righteousness, and it is funny. Don reports that James looks like a man from Mars, with white shorts, a stocking cap, and his glasses tied on with a string. They have taken to carrying their own water from the river, too, instead of buying it. It's a several blocks' trip, and a *tiao* of water is a heavy load. Two buckets, one on each end of a pole over the shoulder. The new mayor is reported to carry his own, and to take his turn at cooking. Living is really being simplified.

Nurse Julie had a good time in Chungking, but was ready to come back. She said she had never seen anything like the hordes of little beggars on the streets. If one wears anything decent, he is bound to be confronted by the young rascals, who use any method from breaking their rice bowls over one's head to smearing one with a handful of fresh mud or throwing a handful of lice into one's hair. This if you refuse to hand over what they ask for. Riding up hill in a ricksha is impossible—too slow and too good an opportunity for the beggars. They follow people into restaurants and sit down at the same table and if the host orders anything different for them than for himself or his guests, they raise a howl. Nobody can handle them at all. The same ones get a tab on certain people, and wait for them each day. One person told of being soundly scolded by a little beggar for not coming out for two days. "How did you think I would eat?" he asked her.

James is back too, and safely. His bus was only robbed once, which is unusual on the big road. Most of them get it three, four, five times between Chengtu and Chungking. A woman was in yesterday (there is a steady stream of them, all with the same story) who is a Christian. She was on her way home, her bus was robbed, and they took everything but the dress she had on and a washbasin. She wasn't a fake, for she had a letter from a friend in Chengtu to us. She said the new government gave all the bus victims their food in Chungking, and bought their tickets for them to the next place.

Oh, dear, the neighbors are home from class, and that is the end of our peace. Just as I guessed, they really are a whole houseful especially chosen to lead songs and sing plays. Their plays are all sung in falsetto, with a very red face and strained neck. They practice every minute they're home. They come along and listen to our choruses when we sing at the church door to invite folks to evangelistic meetings, and then they come home and bellow them to us for the next week, sometimes in not very complimentary revised versions.

This dramatics corps is a powerful cog in the propaganda machine. Through the servants in the rich households, they learn *every* detail about the family's private life. Then they give marvelously accurate take-off performances in huge public meetings. The victim is there by command invitation, and the crowd gets vast enjoyment out of hooting and laughing right to his face.

The play we heard about firsthand dealt with one of Hoch-wan's richest landholders. He was trying to persuade his various wives to sell their valuables and help him pay his exorbitant taxes. But wife number two didn't co-operate. So the landlord seized her only son, the joy of her life, and held him headfirst in a water crock until wifie agreed. You can imagine the glee of the actors and the delight of the mob at a scene like this!

The troops, by the way, have orders not to ask for permission to take time off to go to church. It won't be granted. So now it takes real nerve to come. I don't know why I say troops, for the most of them are just students being indoctrinated. It is more like a youth corps. They are more and more wary of us, but still a few of them drop in. We were saying this week how strange our life is—formerly we longed for a little privacy, and had a hard time getting it. Now it is downright unusual when someone comes in, and it is also difficult for us to go anywhere and be sure we are not embarrassing our friends.

We have talked about a young Christian student named Dzou. He came back after our special meetings, willing to pinch-hit for Gordon while Gordon had a vacation. The vacation fell through, but Dzou is here helping for some weeks anyway. He asked for an audience with us foreign devils the other night—that's what we're called, not what he called us!—and came to deliver his message. He talked for a long time about how he thinks foreigners can best bring the Gospel to the Chinese. He feels that externals are terribly important. Our clothes, our better food, our substantial living quarters, and all the rest. He says that as long as there are these differences between us and them, people only look at and want those *things*. But if someday we can arrive at the point where the only thing we have which they don't have is Jesus Christ, then He will show up in our lives, and they will want Him, too. He says that this is not the day to *preach* the Gospel, but to live it, and of course he is partly right. Nothing he said was news to us, and it is a big problem which we continually work at. But it really struck us anew when he pointed out that when the Word became flesh and dwelt among us, He left a lot more than any of us left. We truly have been too inclined to pat ourselves on the back a little because we live more simply than most foreign establishments we've seen, and we thanked him for the reminders. The mere act of eating bitterness—for its own sake—doesn't mean anything to God, I know, but it surely does to the Chinese, and it gets a contact with them which we'll never get otherwise.

April 2: I'm still waiting for a permit to go home from Chungking. I have had some extra fun and experience by helping E. in the clinic. They are short on doctors—some have gone to Mukden in answer to their appeal for trained personnel; so E. has extra clinic work. She asked me to come and be her secretary; so as she prods around on the patients I write down her dictated reports. All their records are in English, I might add! What a line of pathetic people! She is tops in her department; so those who come to her are the worst cases. People with normal pregnancies just don't see doctors; those who come are always bad off. I don't know why I said I was having "fun"—it really is awful. Venereal disease, cancer, and all the rest. Almost *never* does a mother have all the children she's given birth to—maybe 50 per cent, maybe fewer. A standard question is, "Does your husband go out and 'play' with other women?" And the standard answer is, "of course." They take one or two needles of penicillin, the husband takes none; he keeps on being exposed, and they wonder why the disease doesn't disappear. On the lighter side are patients like one this week who came to say that in fifteen years she'd never borne a child. It came out later in the conversation (quite by accident) that she and her husband have been reunited this week after a separation of fifteen years!

April 10: Still in Chungking, and it is Easter time. Yesterday after English church we took the *Crucifixion* over to E.'s apartment. She was on call all day; so had had no Easter except privately. We enjoyed recorded music till the electricity went off, as it does at least every third night. Then we had supper—eggs scrambled over a tiny charcoal burner, and cinnamon toast made in the fireplace. While we were eating, another friend came bringing a kettle of wet rice—sort of like gruel instead of the usual dry variety—a tiny bit of fish, which is a luxury, and a bowl of soybeans. So we combined our suppers and topped it off with oranges and anagrams. I am more and more convinced that happiness is to be found wherever one wants to look.

E. had a good story to tell. Two days before, she had gone out at night to buy some eggs for a patient who needed extra food and had no money. On her way back, she was holding the eggs cautiously in the square of cloth one carries such purchases in, and she didn't properly protect her pocket. When she got in, her keys were gone. They unlocked a lot of important hospital locks, and contained her name and address; so the thief could find the locks quite easily. Also, they were in a nice leather case, which was worth something. She felt sick. We had given her the case; so she didn't want us to know it was gone. She hunted and hunted but could find no replacement. Nor could she get a key maker to make new keys for her locks. So then she bethought herself of the way pickpockets are organized. She went to the hospital gate and told the gateman her troubles. He went out and got in touch with the head of the local pickpocket ring, announcing that she was willing to pay for her keys back, no questions asked. In half an hour he brought the whole works in, asking $10,000, which in our money is twenty-five cents. All the thief wanted was a little money for food—he wasn't interested in trying to sell the case, for nobody buys such items now. Nor was he interested in trying to break in where he knew the keys would work; that isn't his trade. I'd heard such tales before, but never so firsthand.

Then she told us one of her brother's experiences. He was going somewhere by boat and had to stop over in Shanghai for a day. He knew he didn't dare leave his cabin if he wanted to keep anything; so he went to sleep with his watch under his pillow, but when he awoke it was gone. It was a gift and he prized it. He asked who was the head of the pickpockets around the dock and a man was indicated to him. He approached the man, told his story, and said the watch was very valuable to him personally. Evidently his story impressed the man, for he nodded to a couple of others when they passed by, gave brief instructions, and in a few minutes the watch was returned—without charge!

That called for a retelling of a true story Lady Hoise relates, which topped them all:

A missionary was riding up the Yangtze. While in port he was relieved of a new pair of boots. The Chinese boat captain had been very friendly; so the missionary reported the theft to him. The captain was very much embarrassed and angry that this should happen to his foreign guest. He took immediate action. His boat had a small cannon which he trained on the city hall. Then he sent word in to the mayor that the boots stolen from his boat were to be returned in two hours or the city hall would cease to exist. The clever mayor knew just what to do. He called the two leaders of the city's pickpocket ring to the city hall and told them the situation. Then he locked one of them in the tower and set the other at liberty. You guessed it; in less than two hours the new boots were back!

April 17: The new government is doing a good job of practicing what it preaches, in ways that can't help impressing anyone who has watched previous weak attempts at reform. For instance, last week in just a few days they rounded up 3,900 of the Chungking beggars who were making it almost impossible to venture out. According to the papers, they give them baths and clean clothes, and start teaching them ways to make an honest living. Streets are being widened, daily inspections of places like campuses are really making people clean up their quarters, trees are being planted, and it seems in general that the old system of being a friend of a friend of somebody doesn't help nearly so much.

April 22: Home again to Hochwan. Activities here go on, on a small scale, and with a disheartening and continuous turnover which makes teaching next to impossible. Here today and gone tomorrow. We feel pretty halting and hesitant in taking initiative these days. It somehow doesn't fit into the new plan of things. But over and above the little handicaps and question marks, things keep on happening to assure us of His guidance and presence and blessing. Our being here still seems definitely on the asset side of the ledger. Some situations would go on without pushing, but this is not one of them, nor will it be for a long time. We're glad to be right where we are— that is an unqualified truth.

16. Momentary Millionaires

Was it just because accounting was my field that I found money matters in China so fascinating? I don't think so. When one could send a telegram that cost something over a dollar, and receive in change a twenty-cent piece, a $100,000 bill, and a $20,000 postage stamp, it was, to say the least, unusual. And when we pasted more than 300 stamps on an air form on which was clearly printed "use not more than four stamps," we could safely assume that inflation was here again.

Prices never failed to fascinate us and our friends at home. A $250,000 tube of tooth paste, a three-million-dollar inlay in my tooth, or a check for twenty million sounded impressive until we took our friends to a hundred-million-dollar annniversary dinner.

In our four years in China, we officially used four completely different kinds of money. When we arrived in Shanghai in 1947, Lawrence Burkholder handed us a few thousand each as we walked off the boat toward the customs office. That was CNC, or Chinese National Currency. Our first shopping bags full of it were purchased in Shanghai at CNC $83,000 to U.S. $1, and the last we had on hand a year later when it was finally called in had been purchased at an exchange of more than CNC $7,000,000 to U.S. $1.

That was only the beginning! CNC was replaced by Gold Yuan, coming on the market at a little less than GY $4 to U.S. $1. The following spring we converted our balance on hand at an exchange of GY $27,709,265 to U.S. $1! It had been much, much higher than that—clear up to six hundred million to one, according to an old letter I read. But because we had cashed ours early, the backlog of low exchange pulled down our average.

I was treasurer of our group, and our expense report for the month of May, 1949, read like this:

Expenses:

Equipment	$ 30,335,000
Clothing	7,555,000
Food	2,123,083,000
Household	266,200,000
Building materials	7,272,896,500
Building labor	2,331,616,000
Work supplies	6,000,000
Cables, telegrams, postage	2,457,954,250
Miscellaneous	16,847,000
Gingerich personal	367,136,450
Weaver personal	38,206,250
Bean personal	99,626,050
McCammon personal	825,092,450
Transportation	2,197,040,000
Medical expense, missionaries	100,000,000
Clinic supplies	2,080,300
Servants' wages	252,000,000
Evangelists' wages	392,260,000
Gross expenses:	$18,785,928,250

Income:

Bibles sold	139,000
Clinic	149,239,900
Total income:	$ 149,378,900
Gross expenses	18,785,928,250
less income	—149,378,900
Net expenses:	GY $18,636,549,350

· 126 ·

Believe me, in those days I sent the Board Treasurer an average exchange figure, and let him do the long division! The Chinese adding machine, the abacus, got a lot of good publicity a few years ago when it defeated a modern American calculating machine in a contest staged by some army boys. I never got to the point where I would have chosen it above a Comptometer, but it surely did save me a lot of long columns when the money got wild. And as always, the Chinese were pleased to see us appreciating something of theirs. They learn to use it early in school with the Chinese study technique of memorizing the various combinations by reciting them aloud. I couldn't get it that way, but I could *think* it through; so did. Long division was too hard, but the other three processes worked fine. The only trouble was not having a tape to show how far one was when an interruption came.

After Gold Yuan came silver dollars, starting out more expensive than U.S. dollars, U.S. $1.50 to silver $1. But by the time the new government came, we were buying the best silver dollars for three to U.S. $1. I say "best," for not only was silver currency worth less than hard silver dollars, but some hard ones were worth more than others. The "big heads" were the best, those with a man's head on them, but even their value varied depending on whether the man's eyes were open or shut! There were perhaps half a dozen varieties of "hard" dollars, whose values not only differed from each other, but each one changed daily and sometimes hourly. And there were always counterfeits afloat; so any transaction in silver was accompanied by many ringing sounds as each dollar was clinked against another to hear that it had the same pitch as the last. One merchant would refuse a certain dollar and the next one would unhesitatingly accept it.

The last official currency in which we dealt was of course the People's Government money, or *Jen Ming Pyiao*. JMP came in at more than $20,000 to U.S. $1 and never got over $30,000. When I left I came out cheaply, for my money had all been cashed at $30,000 and exchange was then down to $22,000 again.

Actually those four kinds of money were only about half the story. We always kept a running account in U.S. dollars, and had to think our weird reports back into U.S. to have any idea what we were doing. Then we often had dealings in Hong Kong money, which usually ran about H.K. $6 to U.S. $1. On various occasions when one money was defunct and the next not yet off the press, villages would issue their own local fill-in-the-blank bank notes. And always in reserve were the old-time nickel and copper coins. They came out of hiding every now and then in times of crisis, always revalued. Last but not least were our dealing in thread, not neat round spools of J & P Coats, but big unrefined hanks of gray homespun.

This gives you some idea of the reason why Chinese think in terms of rice, not dollars. A workman is hired for so much rice per day, paid in cash on payday at the latest rice market quotation. He doesn't go home and put the cash away for safe keeping. If he did, it might only buy half as much rice the next morning. Nothing is predictable except the fact that the price will go up, not down; so he buys the salt, sugar, coal, cloth, or other basic commodities he needs, and invests the rest in good safe rice. If he can afford to, he'll eat it. If not, he can always sell it.

The Communist Government was holding prices fairly steady at the time I left China. The way they did it was simple. In each city was one or more large government department stores, selling all the basic necessities of life at fixed prices. One needed only to inquire the price there to know what he could get it for elsewhere—that price less a little. In establishing this control, the government was putting a big crimp in one of the joys of Chinese daily life—bargaining.

Bargaining is fun for everybody. It is a fact that a merchant looked disappointed if a buyer immediately agreed to his price. "How much for this?" we would ask disinterestedly, even if the product was exactly what we wanted and we had secretly determined to have it at any price. "This?" the merchant *always* echoed, thus giving himself time to decide what he dared ask. Then he would name a price about three times the value of the article; we would laugh amusedly, and start to walk away. "Any less or not?" we might call back over a shoulder, but more likely he had already called us back by then. "A little less," or "just to be polite to you," he would smile. And we were off on a bargaining process. He asks a high price; we offer less than we expect to pay. He comes down and we go up slowly. Somewhere in the middle we meet—or perhaps we don't the first time. If it's a major purchase, it may take several visits to the shop to decide who is the slowest to compromise. But no one ever gets angry or impatient. Sometimes we longed for a store where we could ask the price and take it or leave it, but when such stores came to China it didn't feel right at all. And since we're home, we find ourselves tempted to offer a bit less when the price sounds too high!

There is another version of bargaining which women don't indulge in, and that is the up-the-sleeve technique. Don got good at it, and the Chinese men were delighted when he offered to do it. This method is used when the seller doesn't want those gathered around to know the final price agreed on, usually on bigger items of business, and it goes like this: The seller reaches up the long broad sleeve of the buyer and says, "this many tens of thousands" (and he pulls on certain fingers); "this many thousands" (more fingers pulled); "this many hundreds" (another pull), "and this many tens" (final pull). "Ha," laughs the buyer, "that is much too high. I'll give you *this* much." And up the merchant's sleeve goes the buyer's hand, where the same secret process is repeated. Eventually the bargain is reached, and the ubiquitous crowd is more curious than ever.

But now comes the joke, for as the crowd presses close, the

satisfied customer pulls out his sheaf of bills and begins to leaf them off. The crowd counts aloud and watches him hand it over. The satisfied seller pulls out his pouch and makes change, the crowd still calling it out bill by bill. So the party breaks up, with the same result as always—everybody knows everything about everybody else's business—and even more time than usual has been consumed!

17. Days of Decision

The hardest decision our group ever made was agreeing to ask permission to leave China. We had known for months and years that the Communists were coming, but that decision —to stay on—was easy and unanimous. We were never sorry, and these are some of the reasons why. The first six months following our liberation we were not bothered much in our work. In those months Don was able to complete his course of instruction with a number of converts and baptize them. In those months we located a fine young pastor and his wife, both with seminary training, and saw them settled into the work. So far as we know they are still there. It was this pastor who went to Cloud Gate Place and baptized the large group of believers there, after we could no longer leave Hochwan. It was in those months that we were able to encourage the opening of the evangelistic work on "Hit Iron Street," a major area of need in our town. And in all humility may I say that our willingness to stay on and try to enter into the new problems of our small flock helped them to be more calm and less fearful than if we had run when the running was good. We had an ideal situation in those last months to practice what we had been preaching.

I would not for a moment imply that *we* accomplished any of these things; rather we had the sure feeling that God had His hands on us and was using us. As His Word promises, the rewards God gave us far outweighed anything those days may have cost. They came in two forms—we ourselves were drawn closer to Him, and we knew deep joy as we saw others learning to know Him better. I often thought of John's first letter, where he says, "We want you to be with us in this . . . fellowship with God the Father, and Jesus Christ his Son. We must write and tell you about it, because the more that fellowship extends, the greater the joy it brings to us who are already in it."

Here are two intimate insights into some of the details of those days' activities. Had we left early, I could never have written these letters.

"A couple of weeks ago one of our young Christians turned up at Esther's home. They had met when Stockwells visited us, and she had a general idea of where they lived. When she got to their school, there was a conference of several hundred trainees going on, but the man she asked happened to know where they lived, and led her across the campus right to their house. Esther was so surprised she could hardly believe her eyes—L. wore different clothes, of course, and was very thin. But after her first moments of self-consciousness she was glad to talk to Esther and stayed a couple of hours. She was at the end of her training course; they were having a final week of meetings in town and then would be assigned to their jobs. She was in town for the first time, had her evenings free, and was very lonely and unhappy. Then she thought of this home where she could talk freely. She said she had made no attempt to maintain her faith, to pray, or to witness for Christ since leaving home. But with a faith as real as hers had been, she was having a miserable time trying to forget it. Esther admonished her to pray, and helped her remember parts of the Bible she had memorized.

"She was back again in a few days, wanting more help, and feeling more at peace. Then they got the idea that she should talk to us. This girl had been so excited at the possibility of our coming to Chungking that when the prospect faded away she still thought she must talk to us. So Esther telephoned me to say I should call back the following night. We were afraid it wouldn't be too satisfactory; so each of us at Hochwan wrote carefully what we wanted to say to her, and mailed it, hoping she could receive the letter at Esther's when she came to call. I phoned, and got her. I could hear her, but she couldn't hear me; so I just listened. She had a bad conscience about how she'd left. She was afraid we were angry, hadn't forgiven her, and couldn't still love her. She said all this on the phone— some in Chinese and some in English—but couldn't hear my answers! She didn't have our letters. It was almost heartbreaking to hear her little scared voice saying, 'Mrs. Ma, I still remember the Lord is my Shepherd, and I want to come back to Him.' Her only outlet for her faith is this: when they march and sing, L. said they can't hear her anyway; so instead of singing the patriotic songs she sings Sunday-school songs.

"The wonderful end of the story came in Esther's letter a few days later. She said that when they left the phone and went back into the living room, Olin handed them the letters; they had just come! They spent a couple of hours reading them and translating them, looking up the Scripture references, and praying together, and L. went off with a really happy heart, smiling through her tears. She carried our letters and pictures, though she might get in trouble doing it. In my letter, I'd told her clearly all the things she needed to hear me say, beginning with reminders of God's faithfulness. 'If we confess our sins, he is faithful and just to forgive us our sins. . . . ' I went on to the 103rd Psalm, full as it is of assurance of God's tender mercy, and ended with my own sentiment, perfectly expressed by Paul as he wrote to the Thessalonians: 'Because we loved you, it was a joy to us to give you not only the Gospel of God but our very hearts—so dear did you become to us.'

"How happy it has made us all. L. is so naive. She said: 'I hear you need guarantors—I'm writing to my mother to get a list of twenty friends who are willing and bring it to you.' Poor girl, she doesn't know how frightened people are of us up here in the country. Her mother doesn't look at us when she meets us on the street, but I did make bold enough to stop and tell her I'd talked to L., for I know she grieves over her leaving."

❖ ❖ ❖

"I don't tell you much about our work, because it just sort of goes on, and in a small and perhaps to you unexciting way. But truly these are days in which the Lord is helping us—almost *making* us—grow. That doesn't mean it's all pleasant or easy. We all have an abnormal share of growing pains, but I think we welcome them more than we ever did before. I'm especially grateful for times when He lets us enter into other people's problems, and uses us to help them even a little. I've had a couple of afternoons this very week which I wouldn't trade for anything, and which would have made coming to China and learning Chinese completely rewarding if I had to go home tomorrow. It's times like that when I feel at the same time most humble and most happy. It is, of course, when the Lord really uses us in down-to-earth situations that we can feel like that.

"This time it was Julie. She and I are over the racial and language barriers about as well as anybody I've yet known in China. We can understand and forgive each other remarkably well. And so we can get into some pretty involved discussions, well over both of our heads, and beyond our experiences spiritually. She has an unusually good mind, and with it needs to learn to be humble. It isn't easy. From a baby up, people have helped her be proud and sure of her ability. I'm no shark with the language, nor do I handle my Bible as I'd like to, but it is certainly thrilling to see how God gives one what he needs at times like this. This week we've been able to read and think and talk and pray together, to say things that are awfully hard to get out, to admit to God things that are awfully necessary but hurt terribly, and today we both have a deeper, more unshakable faith and happiness than ever before, because we have a clearer vision of where our strength lies. 'I can do all

· 134 ·

things *through Christ. . . .* ' 'Be strong *in the Lord,* and in the power of *his* might.' '*My God* shall supply all your needs. . . .' Verses like that, and many more of them, at times of need like hers, just simply pick people up and set them on solid ground. It shakes them, but it doesn't hurt them—just leaves them less sure of themselves (which is fine) and more sure of Him who is able to do 'exceeding abundantly above all that we ask or think. . . . ' And when God is good enough to let me be there to watch and maybe help a bit, I wouldn't trade places with anybody."

But even as we rejoiced in these individual opportunities which were still ours, we began to be forced to question the wisdom of staying on. Friends whose opinions we valued, quietly advised us to leave. Our first reaction was to think the advice was solely for our own good. Then we began to wonder whether they wished it for their sakes! We grew almost overly sensitive to the turned head and the downcast eye as we met friends on the street, and had to check to see how much we were imagining. There was plenty of evidence left after we eliminated the possible imaginings! We followed the news as best we could, and tried to formulate some minimum require-ments for an evangelistic program worth promoting. What if we were openly forbidden to teach or preach Christ? Men-nonitism is peculiarly a "way of life," but *only* to live it. . . ? What if we were absolutely cut off financially—could we take it? What if this new doctrine which was invading every area of Chinese life crept into the church program, and it became a choice between including it or not preaching? How would our leaving affect our own small family of Christians? These and endless other questions surged through our minds day and night. One day we would reach a decision; the next morning one of us would be unsure of the wisdom of it.

Finally in July of 1950 we four Hochwanites concluded that our presence was clearly becoming a handicap to our fellow workers and the other Christians, and so we made application for exit permits. We had lived under the Communists since early December of 1949, and by July their propaganda machine was going full blast and producing excellent results. If I had not been there to experience it, I would never have believed that in a few months the liberators could so effectively have touched every life. Slow-moving, illiterate, unwieldy, rural old China, steeped in tradition and superstition, had seemed to me a most unpromising candidate to be reformed and remodeled by the vigorous young liberators. But it happened! In those few months every last household was aware of the change. Through endless meetings where attendance was carefully checked, they had heard over and over the new doctrines. Through public trials they had seen demonstrated the simple techniques for evening old scores—one accuser was enough now. Through mass executions, at which time even grade schools were dismissed and young pupils required to attend, they had seen the quick death which awaited those who refused to "change their thoughts." In the months that followed they and we saw the long-awaited land reform, and the loosely controlled goings on in those days only heightened the sense of fear which already pervaded every household and governed every thought and action. By then husband and wife feared to speak confidentially to each other and both were careful of their remarks when the children were home. Nothing was considered more glorious than to report one's own relatives for reactionary thinking or other questionable conduct. Nobody discussed affairs outside the home. An intelligent Chinese friend actually said to me, "You should take the newspapers and read them carefully. Then you would know what you may talk about."

The day we filed our applications for exit permit was not a happy one. It was a major turning point in our small mission's history, and it wasn't turning the way we had hoped and prayed it might. We had met the attack; now we were withdrawing, and it was a bitter pill to swallow. God mercifully gave us wisdom even then to see that we were quite dispensable, and humility enough to be thankful for the fact! Our withdrawal was by no means the withdrawal of His church, even in our own field. We could no longer cope effectively with the enemy in that place, but He could, He is, and He shall!

Months later we were still waiting for action on our applications. Our work was different in those days; it was a work of intercession, of appropriation, of bearing the silent fruits of the Spirit. We had much time for reading, for pondering, for personal inventory. Thanksgiving came, and at first thought it seemed a strange holiday. Then we took time, and found more than ever to be thankful for. Some words I wrote that day voice something of what I've tried to express in this chapter.

THANKSGIVING—1950

Thanksgiving Day again. A day on which
To cast through this year's memory store
And turn in thanks to Thee for what I find.

I wrote it last year too, this Hymn of Thanks;
Nice-sounding words, well rhymed, and from my heart,
But somehow childish, and a public thing.

This year I know Thee better. And the thanks
I bring are deeper, harder wrought, more real;
The fruits of sifting, searching all Thou'st sent.

This year I tasted fear in my own heart,
And doubt; and worse, the sense of being feared!
Frustration, utter helplessness, deep pain.

I sampled for the first the bitter cup
Of seeing dear friends in the throes of strife
And having neither strength to give, nor word.

I stood and watched a curtain coming down
Upon a land I love. I heard them say
The harsh, the awful truth, "You cannot share."

I heard Thy name confessed and then denied;
I saw weak creatures trust themselves and fall.
I caught a glimpse of what Thy church must face.

But more, I caught a clearer glimpse of Thee!
Of power Thou giv'st to those who pray in faith!
Of peace reserved for all who seek Thy rest!

Thyself Thou hast shown strong at every turn,
In strength'ning, vital, overpowering love,
And ever will, to all who name Thy name!

   Thanks be, Great God, to Thee!

18. "The Leveling Process"

The general subject of taxation was number one conversation topic among the Chinese until people no longer talked so freely. It was also of real interest to foreigners all over China and some of them had drastic firsthand experiences. Tax evasion or charges of misrepresentation were common "accusations" in the latter days, and we were relieved to get out of China without any serious difficulties on this score. No Chinese landholder was that fortunate.

The first step of the program designed to ruin all landholders concerned what we call "key money." In old China a landlord may have tens or hundreds of tenants, and each one had paid a certain deposit apart from the regular rent. If one tenant left, his fee was refunded by the landlords but was immediately collected from the new tenant. Now came an order for *all* landlords to refund *all* key money to *all* tenants immediately—the custom was abolished. The mere calculation of the total fees involved was a nightmare, for they had been paid in all sorts of different moneys. The payment was often an impossibility for the landlord, because he couldn't sell land to get cash. Nobody would buy!

Rather than have it appear that the government was being so rough, the clever officials gave authority to the farmers' union to see that this was satisfactorily settled. Things went completely wild. Many landlords were killed, more were tortured, others imprisoned, and very few escaped the experience of at least having their homes raided and their personal treasures taken. Many, including some gentle old ladies, had only the garments they wore when it was finished. Afterward the government took things back in hand again, but not until they were satisfied with the damage done.

The next blow came in taxes themselves. Tremendous taxes were levied on the landholders, and he who couldn't pay was again punished severely. The prisons were so full by then that extra buildings had to be used temporarily.

The final "leveler" came in the actual land reform program. Then it was that the land was taken from the owner and given out in tiny parcels to the poor. It was apportioned according to the number in the family who could work it and the number of mouths there were to feed. The landlord was included in the dividing if he wished; he could have a piece too, the size to be determined on the same basis. So the rich were now poor, the poor still poor, and the very poor a bit better off. That was the equalizing process, under which as one skeptic put it, "all men are equal, but some are more equal than others."

Protestant missions we knew of didn't suffer too much injustice through this era. The much-hated Catholics were often victimized because they had much of their money invested in land. Protestants didn't have tenants; so the key-money ruling didn't apply. In the case of tax assessments, we and those we knew of paid a good-sized tax, but not really ridiculously unfair. Our land was not seized for redistribution, because we didn't have that kind of land. The final responsibility for tax assessment in our neighborhood rested on a local committee. Total taxes which the city had to produce were announced, then it was broken down into smaller groups until eventually each small neighborhood unit knew how much its share was.

Very tiresome to us was the endless measuring of our property. I won't even venture a guess at how many times an excited group of neighbors rushed in with a string or long rag and measured our lot, counted our rooms, and tried to classify the buildings according to what they were built of. Our deed and title with all that information on it was often gone for weeks at a time, but we did get it back every time except the last.

The red tape connected with closing the clinic caused us more trouble. In that instance we had to stretch our imaginations to feel that we received fair treatment. We closed in August, since we thought we were leaving and Nurse Julia was going away to school. In September we received a tax assessment which seemed very high, since it was based on clinic income and our income was very low because of our nonprofit motive. Inquiry disclosed that our actual tax for January to August was only half that much, but because we had failed to file certain forms when we stopped operating the clinic, they also taxed us for the nonoperating month of September, and the charge for that one month was as much as for the first eight months, though they knew we had not received a penny!

Be sure that we then got our forms and *officially* closed the clinic. Then began discussions of what should be done with the medicines and other supplies. They warned us that we dared not dispense so much as a pill after going out of business. In fact, they were so vehement in their warnings that we offered to store the whole works with them, reserving the right to get supplies which one of our own mission family might need. No response. Then we learned that they really wanted our medicines to *use,* not to store; so we offered them. But that direct approach struck them too much as American charity to poverty-stricken China; so they wouldn't accept. A good bit of useful and valuable medicine went to waste because of their pride. At the same time they descended on our CIM friends and *demanded* their medicines, though they weren't even operating a clinic, nor had they been! Their medicines were mostly German homeopathic supplies which were totally unfamiliar to the Chinese. In an effort to prevent real trouble and danger from misused medicines, Irmtrud poured some of the strongest mixtures down the drain!

How slow we were to learn! Had we acted reluctant and unco-operative our medicines would doubtless have been taken and used. As it was, our eagerness only angered the authorities, and the medicine molded quietly past its usable date. We weren't surprised at any of this, nor should you be. Here is a translated sample of what the Chinese were reading those days from Chairman Mao's pen:

"At this point, I think it necessary to call people's attention to the fact that the imperialists and their running dogs, the Chinese reactionaries, will not take their defeat in China lying down. They will still work in collusion with each other and use all possible means to oppose the Chinese people. They will, for example, send their lackeys to bore into China to carry out work of disintegration and disruption. This is inevitable and they will certainly not forget this work. They will, for instance, egg on the Chinese reactionaries, or may, in addition, even come out with their own forces to blockade the seaports of China. They will do this if it is still possible for them to do so. Furthermore, if they want to be adventuristic, the sending of part of their armed forces to encroach on China's frontiers is not an impossibility. We must fully take all this into account. We must decidedly not, because of our victories, relax our vigilance toward the wild retaliatory plots of imperialist elements and their running dogs. Whoever relaxes such a vigilance will be politically disarmed and be placed in a passive position. Under these circumstances, people throughout the country must unite and smash firmly, thoroughly, cleanly, and completely all the antipopular conspiratorial schemes of the imperialists and their lackeys . . . China must be independent . . . the affairs of China must be decided on and dealt with by the Chinese people themselves, and not the slightest intervention by any imperialist country is allowed . . . ."

There was no question what the new leaders thought of our country. Now add to this opinion the rumor that we were really representing our government, and see why people were more than a little leery of us. I wrote home that month: "We are grateful to be allowed the freedom we have to move about and preach and teach. And we surely must work while it is day . . . . Against the present background, the new-found joy and peace of those who are hearing and believing shines even brighter, and makes everything about life seem more worth while. Analyses of work like this can't be made in any man-devised statistics, but take our word for it, the results are gratifying beyond expression."

19. "A Mary a Christmas"

Christmas in this country is doubtless over-commercialized, but the spirit of the season is entered into by many, and the true meaning of Christmas is at least understood by all.

In a country where only one per cent of the population professes faith in Christ, the season celebrating His birth is naturally not nearly so well known. In more cosmopolitan coastal cities like Shanghai there was quite a general flurry of decorating; in the university towns like Chengtu there was an unfortunate overemphasis on the necessity of giving gifts; in the rural areas like Hochwan, Christmas was not known except as Christ was known.

It is hard to imagine four more different seasons than our four China Christmases. They seem to me significant enough to share with you. The first, on the campus in Chengtu, reflects our unthinking acceptance of and participation in the long-practiced rituals between "inferiors" and "superiors." They bowed much and gave little; we bowed little and gave much. Everybody felt warm for the moment but we ate the goose. God forgive us and help us to learn. The second Christmas came only a few weeks after our arrival at our country station. It was a complete farce, staged solely in deference to us. Nobody felt very warm that year. The third year brought a truly joyous first Christmas to the fine group of new Christians who had found Christ in Hochwan. There we had Christmas as it is meant to be! Our last Christmas season found most young people scattered, and fear everywhere. The "celebrating" was mainly in individual hearts, for neither we nor they dared take the initiative in any announced festivities. But to all who had clung to Him during the past difficult year, this

Christmas was the most meaningful of them all, for externals were stripped away and Christmas was Christ!

"Christmas shopping has been simple, but at that it wasn't exactly easy to think of and find things. I found a pair of big enough fur-lined gloves for Don, after much hunting for dress gloves. He also needed warmer everyday ones; so I hied myself to a shop where they make them, but they had none big enough. They said they'd make a pair of nice big fur-covered ones for about $1 gold. Another enterprise I undertook was to get a 'chop' made for Don. The Chinese have long, rectangular, stone sticks with the characters for their names written on the ends. They dip the end into a sort of sealing-wax mixture, and 'chop' it on important documents. You can imagine my fun in both of these negotiations with people who don't know a scratch of English—we've been here two months! It's good exercise for my Chinese, though. I had a literate ricksha boy that day, who was a lot of help.

"Christmas Day was a rainy one, but quite perfect for sitting by a roaring fire; so we did. We have fireplaces in every room in the house, but it was the first fire we have had, since fuel is so high. Ordinarily we make one heating stove do for everybody. After breakfast Bill, our host, called the servants in for their gifts. For some reason they seemed quite prepared for such a 'surprise,' and were all congregated in the kitchen. But the coolie came without his wife, and had to go to the kitchen for her; and she came without the little girl, and we had to send for her. They are very careful not to step out of bounds, it seems. They all lined up in the living room, and Bill made a little talk about Christmas. He told the coolie that he would be interested in how Jesus was born, since he kept cows and had a stable, but Bill thought probably the stable Jesus came to was a bit cleaner! Then in a very nice way he told the story simply, in their own

11

language. He told them how we appreciated their work, and how he couldn't teach and we couldn't go to school if it wouldn't be for their work of keeping things going well at home. Next we handed them their gifts from under the tree, and they bowed and bowed and were awfully sweet. We gave them all some little material things, but mostly money, for they know best what they need. They had given the household a goose for dinner. We gave the cook money for glasses, hoping thereby to eliminate a few hairs and other impurities from the food. A few days later his wife came in wearing them! You see, they were called reading glasses, and she was the only member of the family who could read!

"After that came our own gifts, and I wouldn't be surprised if I were the only one in our family to receive a package worth an even million—I see by the expense sheet that that's what Don spent on it. That's about $7 this week, by the way. It bought eight lovely silver napkin rings, a very pretty and well-made silver tea strainer, and a pair of simply beautiful filigree silver bud vases. Their filigree work is exquisite. Silver seems to be Chengtu's specialty. We exchanged names in our Mennonite group, and the two girls who had Don's and my name gave us butter spreaders. I gave Don his gloves and 'chop.' Besides this we had several small things among the household and neighborhood. Then after a visit with the girls for a while, it was time to set the table. Our place cards were Medici prints from England. Christine, Ruth, Luella, a Chinese professor whose wife didn't get back, and a Friends Ambulance Unit boy were our guests. So we had China, Canada, the States, and England represented. Bill swallowed his good Quaker principles and asked Don to say grace—the first spoken grace we've had here! I'm sure we all thought of our missing families, but since we all had the same lacks, nobody gave anybody else an opportunity to feel homesick, thank goodness.

"The dinner was delicious, with the goose done to perfection. Bill said that in lieu of any formal entertainment, he would carve—he hates to! We had fresh peas and carrots, fresh spinach, potatoes about like oversized French fries, dressing and gravy, applesauce and homemade bread. Our dessert was a giant steamed pudding with good tart lemon sauce. Then we moved to the fire and had tea and an assortment of fudge and stuffed dates that we girls had made the night before. We sent Don out to find cocoa for our fudge, and he came back with a one-pound can that cost $140,000! Rather steep, but it was Christmas Eve! The candy was a great treat to everyone, and we consumed an amazing quantity.

"The day before, I had asked Bill if he would read Dickens' 'Christmas Carol,' and he said he didn't have it in the house, but if I could 'scrounge' it, he would 'Scrooge' it; so I did and he did, to perfection. The party broke up by candlelight, for it was a 'dark' night (no electricity every third night). Then Don and I went out for a walk. We had a slippery walk all right, but it was mud instead of ice. Exactly the same problem of keeping our balance, however, since the roads are clay and they are a fright when they're wet. We spent a quiet evening of talk around the fire, and the day was over about the time yours was beginning.

"It has been interesting to see the way some Chinese people, to whom Christmas doesn't mean anything, personally, very carefully take care of their obligations to the foreigners anyway. It is so well calculated as to amount to a business transaction. The gifts arrive very early from social 'inferiors,' for they are to be repaid three or four times the value of what they send, and people who have no business in the world sending things just 'cash in' on the big day. Bill received baskets and baskets of oranges, all of which are good currency, for all the carolers expect to be fed. The cakes they have made are quite fantastic; Bill received three from various groups, done up with everything from huge roses and 'A Mary a Christmas' to a log with toadstools.

"We tried going to a Chinese church service last week, but the only thing we received from the service was near-pneumonia; it lasted a full two hours, in a place quite like a tomb, with us properly dressed for Sunday after a week of wool stockings, long underwear, stadium boots, and the rest. I thought I'd die before we finally left. The main reason we went was to hear the Christmas music, which really was delightful.

"On Christmas Eve there were ever so many groups out caroling. They send notices ahead to folks whom they'll visit, which is to say, 'Please prepare tea, cakes, and tangerines.' The prettiest group of all was the student nurses, dressed in white uniforms, caps, and shoes, with their red-lined capes on inside out, and carrying bamboo torches. Another beautiful pre-Christmas program we enjoyed was at the Canadian mission girls' high school. Excellent singing and the costumes for the pageant were exquisite as only Chinese silks and Chinese artists could make them."

1948

"Another Christmas down in history, and a lively chapter it makes. Ruth just called out and said she wished I'd write my book soon—she wants something interesting to read! You see what we think of our existence. . . . Anyway, we have fun and keep happy. No Christmas mail at all; so in an effort to help things, I used my pull at the post office. I have an English Bible student there who always says, 'What seek ye?' when I go in! I got them to deliver the mail at night instead of the next morning, and now the girls all hate me because they say I killed the goose that laid the golden egg; they have nothing to look forward to in the morning! Christine was the smart one; she left all her Christmas notes till after Christmas and was just going to answer what she got. Now she doesn't have a lick of work to do!

"Where to start? We drew names among ourselves, and

stood on our heads in our barrels doing our Christmas shopping. None of that crowded department store stuff for us. Almost we didn't buy anybody anything. I had asked for money to be transmitted days and weeks ago, but it didn't come. I hated to wire again, and finally we didn't have money enough to wire. Came December 23, and we had used not only our own but all of our teacher's money, the cook's, and the German ladies'. And still there were workmen to pay and a several-hundred-dollar feast to pay for at the orphanage the next day! I had decided to phone Chungking; the bank said they'd stake me to the ninety dollars it cost. I sat there all afternoon, at least four hours, and finally the telephone office said they guessed they were out of order—couldn't get Chungking! I was desperately trying to sell them a U.S. $20 bill we had, or borrow money from them, but could do neither. I came home, and rounded up the last $10 we had for a five-word telegram. Three words were address and one signature; so the message simply said, 'desperate.'

"About dark came a delegation of men from the bank. One had tried to go to another bank to sell my U.S. bill, and they said there that $5,000 had come there for some foreign name, but they didn't know who we were! So they brought an official along and he wanted me to write all of our names. I did. He shook his head, 'No.' I said it *had* to be 'Yes'! He said, 'No, it says Mrs. Donald McCammon, and you didn't write Donald; you wrote Don'! To make a long story shorter, we finally got the cash the next day, and meanwhile the bank boys brought money yet that night out of their own funds, and the cook went out after dark and bought meat and vegetables for the orphanage. The next morning we felt really Christmasy to see the little 'goo-ers' come with baskets on their back and with shining eyes carry off loads almost bigger than themselves of rice, meat, greens, soybean curd, and oranges.

"We had a terribly long program on Christmas Eve at the church, another long one on Christmas morning, climaxed with a feast of all the church members dining together, as our guests, at the pastor's suggestion. We thought it most remarkable for the old pastor to produce members whom we had never seen before or have never seen since, to give speeches for hours on Christmas Eve, and continue full speed on Christmas morning. We had some sort of performance by almost every member of the audience. Don spoke briefly but well; the girls did nobly as the three wise (wo)men, and I escaped. We had everything from testimonies to a magician, from at least ten short sermons to a comedian.

"We were not very happy as we returned from the physically and spiritually cold atmosphere and thought of those who had rambled pointlessly, sung funny songs, and even done acrobatics. But Christmas night as we sat by our own fire and listened to a complete recording of the 'Messiah,' our minds turned to that Messiah whose name we have come to proclaim and our hearts were warmed. We thought of home but we rejoiced that we were permitted to be here."

1949

"*Dec. 20:* Don and I wrapped gifts. We girls made candy and packed two lovely boxes that looked as though they were right off the shelf of a Fannie May store. But when we tried to mail them to Stockwells and a Chinese friend, the post office said it could only accept letters. Obliging Don got up early next morning and persuaded someone on the steamer to take them down. The servants gave us a *tyiao* (two bushels) of tangerines and a chicken.

"*Dec 24:* Last-minute wrapping and decorating. Ruth has supervised the teen-age group in making a really beautiful large-size manger scene, and Christine has been helping them make pretty decorations for the tree. In the evening we had a public program of singing and reading of the Christmas story. The church was packed and overflowing. Then after church the servants and all co-workers had dessert, songs, and gifts together. A whole parade of nice people with tiny sensible gifts today, which makes us happy.

"*Dec. 25:* Everybody in the proper spirit and the coffee even extra good. Good attendance, singing, sermon, and spirit at church. In the P.M. the orphanage children had special permission to come in for Sunday school. Big meeting all together, with the church running over again. Each class sang, Gordon told the Christmas story with flannelgraph materials, and we gave out a lovely Christmas card to each child. The English words were cut off and a Chinese verse printed on. I wish people could see the joy not only children but well-educated adults get from those old cards. They look a lot more beautiful to us from here, too!

"*Dec. 26:* Sent all the supplies for a specially good dinner to the orphanage this morning. This P.M. a group of indignant little youngsters came hot-footing in to tell us that their higher-ups had appropriated most of the supplies, and they didn't even 'eat full.' It is true, and we were so ired by it that we bought another fifty pounds of meat and some vegetables and sent it out for their supper. This nasty official had already come back to town, thinking the show was over. This was probably the wrong technique, but certainly was doing what comes naturally. Is there anything lower than taking food from children who only eat like that once a year? The same fellow wouldn't let them put up a Christmas tree which several little boys skipped dinner to go after. Scrooge the second!"

1950

"This was our second Christmas season under Communism. Our decorations, food, gifts, and cards were all more local products than ever before, but it was fun. Gradually we have used up about everything, or else given it away when we thought we were going. We had children's Sunday-school program on Sunday afternoon, with more than 100 children. (Ruth went; the rest of us didn't.) Then Sunday evening we had a prayer meeting for the Christians, and the Christmas Day church service was an evangelistic meeting to which all Christians had invited friends and neighbors. There were perhaps thirty-five there; lately our church has been averaging fifteen to twenty. Last year the church was full.

"On December 24 the CIM girls had us for Swedish Christmas Eve. First a delicious smorgasbord, with ham, tongue, and liverwurst, all home-cured. Then huge bowls of rice porridge with cinnamon, milk, and sugar. None of us ever found the lonely almond supposedly swimming therein. It is a sign that the finder will be married within the new year, Thali (rhymes with jolly) says. After that they lit the candles on their tree, and we sat by the fireplace and sang carols. Guess where my mind was, as I drank in that lovely fire! It was soon time to go home (we are supposed to be in before the night watchman bongs his bell the second time), but before we left we had good coffee and a whole round of Swedish pastries, most of which we carried home because we couldn't eat them and wouldn't leave them! On Christmas night we had those girls for high tea, at which time Christine performed her usual miracle of pretty and tasty things to eat. We used the last of our candles, some evergreen branches, and our imaginations to dress up the living room attractively. Yesterday we finished off our festivities by having the servants for dinner, and entertaining our Chinese colleagues from both churches at tea. Today we are eating leftovers, and hoping that our digestive tracts will soon be back to normal.

"Running all through this week has been the drawn-out process of registering for residence permits. The foreigners in Chungking did it last January, but it had never come here till now. Finally the forms were all finished to turn in, and the time came for interviews. This was to be by two's—Christine and I on Sunday, and Don and Ruth on Christmas Monday. The official is a northerner, and we were a bit apprehensive about our understanding him, but we certainly had a pleasant surprise. Christine and I talked with him more than an hour at church time on Sunday, and it was purely a delight. He was thoughtful and considerate and courteous at every turn. On Christmas Don and Ruth went, and Christine and I thought they were a long time coming home. But when they came in, they'd had just as nice a time; so we had a two o'clock egg sandwich, grilled on our living room heating stove for Christmas dinner, and were grateful.

"There is one lad who fails to see the light, and keeps coming to visit. Christmas brought a roast duck which likely cost half his month's salary, and this note: 'Wish you have a happy Christmas. Here we present to you a roast duck. To instead of the roast goose or turkey for your Christmas dinner. Though it is a poor gift but with our hearty faithful emotion to you.'"

20. Our Faith Is Tested

We had felt that our usefulness to the Chinese church was finished. After several months of stalling, bluffing, and outright lying, the local officials revealed that they still wanted to make use of us a bit before letting us go. They needed some well-fed living examples of what they had been teaching their people to hate above all else—Americans!

In July, 1950, Don had unwittingly offended some neighboring soldiers. It was his custom to keep our new compound wall cleared, and he had several small signs hung there which said in Chinese "please post no bills." Unfortunately, the three small illegible (to him) posters which he tore down one day said "Congratulations to the Communist Party." We think they were put there in the hopes that he would take them down. He was the only foreign man in town, and they were looking for any slight excuse to make trouble for him. When he learned that some soldiers had turned in a formal accusation, he took the advice of Chinese friends and presented a written apology. That was only the beginning! After thirty-some trips to inquire about the delay in our exit permits, he learned that his apology was unacceptable, and presumably it was for that reason that our permits were not forthcoming. Then began a series of rewording and padding that apology—now it was all right but this phrase, now this meaning should be a little clearer, etc., ad inf.! Always these corrections required the services of an expert Chinese writer, which services were rapidly becoming more difficult to secure.

This incident will show you that the new government is not

without its weakness. In the old days in China, it was a standing joke and an actual fact that all one needed was a friend, or a friend of a friend, to accomplish anything. Under the liberators "pull" supposedly did no good. A friend of a friend of ours was a big shot in the city government. He was a perfect stranger to us, but at our friend's request he inquired for us what the holdup was. Promptly the word came that we could leave. Don came home jubilant with our permits in his pocket. But that night about midnight came a pounding on the gate. Don was sick; so I took a flashlight and unbarred the gate. There were several red-star soldiers demanding to see the permits. You can be sure I was reluctant to hand them over, but there was no alternative. They pointed out to me a place where they had been written incorrectly, and insisted on taking them back, promising that the next day we would receive corrected ones. Of course we never did, but we learned that the friend of our friend left town early the next day on a long trip; so he was not immediately aware of the development. His request had in a sense been granted, and he would know enough not to ask again when he saw what the score was. This scrap from a home letter expresses our outlook then:

"Waiting is wearisome business. We have very little to do, and the less we go out the better; so the days and nights seem awfully long sometimes. Christine sighed this week and said, 'I wonder if anybody will ever seem interesting again!' We still love each other, but when none of us is away at all, and we all read the same things and meet the same people, there's not much new! Ruth and I, after Christine's remark, took a fling at the 'Holy City,' and the whole family laughed when we discovered that the first chorus we'd got ourselves into said:

'No shadows yonder! All light and song!
Each day I wonder, and say, "How long
Shall time me sunder from that dear throng?"

'No weeping yonder! All fled away!
While here I wander each weary day,
And sigh as I ponder my long, long stay.' "

Almost six months and several repackings later, three soldiers came to tell Don that the officials wanted to see him. When he went for his coat they held the door open, never letting him get out of their sight. We sensed that he was under arrest, though we didn't know why. Then they told him to leave his keys, that he wouldn't be needing them, and one guard outside told the servants to bring a bedroll later. When he left I had no idea when we would meet again, but in a few hours a little messenger came to say that we could send food to him. The cook said he'd take it, but acting on a hunch I said I'd go. Imagine our mutual amazement and joy when I was politely ushered into Don's tiny cell! In the days that followed, I was allowed to take his food and talk to him in Chinese. After that first visit I was not permitted to enter his cell and always I was required to taste all his food before he ate it. It seems that a more devoted wife would have poisoned him, thus causing those who arrested him to lose much face, and perhaps saving him from torture and punishment.

The next day was Sunday and we surprised everyone by attending church services as usual. It turned out to be the last Chinese worship service we did attend. After church I took Don's first meal of the day—he had suggested eating on a two-meal-a-day schedule as his bayonet-toting guards did—and he said he had simply frozen all night. Buildings in our part of China were never heated; so when it got down to 28 degrees one felt pretty chilly. I recalled that a few weeks before when we had been looking at curios on secondhand street, Don had tried on a Chinese fur-lined gown that came nearer fitting him than most; so I hunted up the shop, bought the gown for JMP $300,000 (about $10 U.S.), and took it to him. Before I got home I met one of the other girls from our group hunting for me. A delegation of officials wanted to see me right away, and the frightened girls were sure I was about to be arrested too. When I got home our little breezeway sitting room was filled with not only the official visitors, but our Chinese evangelistic workers, those of the other Protestant mission in town, and all the Christians who could be rounded up on short notice. The chairman had taken a little drink to brace him for this ordeal, I think. Red-faced and wild-eyed, he proceeded to pull from his pocket a Chinese newspaper and read aloud an account of how the Chinese in America were being treated. He then said that naturally we would be treated in the same way, hence from that moment on our funds would be frozen and our personal property sealed until it could be thoroughly inventoried. He then added a variation of his own to the anti-American theme by telling me, with his face a very few inches from mine, how dishonest we were. When the show was finished—the Christians properly impressed, you can know—the lesser officials stayed to watch as we removed the necessities of living from our desks, dressers, cupboards, closets, etc., and then sealed all of these with paper strips and warned us not to break the strips. It took most of a week to complete this inventory. I recall that they began in the kitchen, where they listed 12½ pairs of chopsticks and even three empty jars, but several weary days later the attraction had worn off and they were merely writing "one trunk of personal effects." From that time until we left it was necessary for us to present each month a slip of paper saying how much money we wanted to draw from our bank account, plus statistics on how many bars of soap, cans of fruit, etc., we had used the past month. It was a bit of bother but they never raised questions and always affixed the necessary "chop" to our check.

But to go on with Don's story. Next day was January 1, and a big holiday as New Year's Day has always been in China. Don was told that he would meet some officials to discuss his apology. He had written one in English again as soon as they put him in jail. But when they led him out several blocks away, he soon discovered that it was no small committee meeting he was attending. He was marched to the public parade grounds, where several thousand spectators were listening to speeches. He was required to stand at attention on the rear of the platform; they adjusted his hands and feet to their liking. When the speaker was finished Don was introduced. He was supposed to tell who he was, where he came from, and what his "crimes" were, but each time he started to speak he was drowned out by organized "cheers" among the soldiers. He always gets a laugh when he tells how the yells were against Truman, MacArthur, and McCammon, and he got the loudest ones!

Then the meeting turned into one of the famous "People's Courts." The chairman asked the crowd what to do with this renegade, and again careful planning was apparent as the soldiers and those in workers' uniforms raised their right hands and shouted, "Shoot him!" "That's a serious judgment," said the chairman on the public-address system. "Are you sure that's what you want?" And again the crowd raised their hands and cried, "Shoot him!" "If that is the people's will," intoned the chairman, "it shall be done." So Don was led off to prison again, fully believing that he was condemned to be shot. When he reached his cell, he was carefully locked in for the first time, the main gate of the building was closed, and a big timber pushed against the door. The guard who had previously sat nonchalantly in the hall now stood at attention with his gun ready.

Don says that in those hours the presence of Christ with him was more real than that of the guards marching him through the streets. I was proud when a Chinese who attended the trial told a missionary friend that Don's acceptance of his sentence was magnificent—he didn't even turn pale. He was not at all afraid to die, only terribly sad to leave me and his unborn child. Weeks later we heard that his home church was having a special prayer meeting for us *at the very hour of his trial.* They had no idea of the nature of our need, but they felt prompted of God's Spirit to pray, and did so. And so we don't wonder how we endured those hours; we *know* from whence our strength came.

Several hours later an official came to him and asked if he understood what had been said. Not wanting to believe it, Don said he wasn't sure. "You're to leave the country immediately," said the comrade. "That isn't what they said out there," Don said; "I understood them." "Oh," laughed the comrade, "we wouldn't do that to you. Those people don't know how to deal with foreigners. You are leaving immediately." And he did. He tried then in good Chinese fashion to "bargain." He would gladly be imprisoned if we girls could be allowed to go. But that was one time when the Chinese didn't care to bargain. When I took his supper that evening, he had prepared a list of things for me to put into the one suitcase he was allowed. Another comrade went along home with me and opened seals so that I could get things out. Ironically enough Don had to pay his own fare! It took about a third of our total cash, and we were not at all sure whether we were getting any more. There was a check to cash in transit, but whether it got cashed before this "freezing" order we weren't to know for several weeks. Ostensibly for that reason, but partly because I needed to share my grief with a dear friend, I asked permission to phone long distance and inquire about said check. The guard went with me, and made me talk to this foreign friend in Chinese. If any operators were listening in that night, I imagine they are still laughing. I am sure it was the world's dumbest conversation, but my purpose was accomplished. Next day Esther called me, and we talked more intelligently in English. She could know my heart, for her husband had been taken two months earlier.

Next morning early we three girls went to the riverside, and sure enough here came the prisoner and his guard. A hurried good-by kiss and then the guard ordered him on board and me to go back. Again I had no idea where or whether we would meet again on this earth, but we both had assurance from God that we could take what came.

In that moment at the boat the guard had allowed me (after carefully scrutinizing it upside down) to give Don a note in which I had written some of the things I couldn't speak. One of these was to share with him the first verse of Psalm 34. It had kept getting in my way as I tried to find comfort in God's Word early that morning and finally I had accepted it as for us both. It says, "I will bless the Lord at all times: his praise shall continually be in my mouth."

My next word came about ten days later in a letter from Don which somehow got mailed. It was his third to me, but the only one which arrived. In it he said he was somewhere in the mountains near Chungking, but thought he really was being sent out soon. About three weeks later came a wonderful wire from him, "Arrived Hong Kong safely last night." It was months before I could know the rest of the story. After being held three days in Chungking, he was marched at gun point through the streets of the city, then taken up eight or nine miles into a lonely mountainous section where the carriers were dismissed by the guards and again he thought his time had come to leave this world. Instead he soon found himself in an old police-training camp where he was confined to a tiny room for nine days, with coarse food and always cold, but never harmed in any way except for heckling. Then back to the city again, and this time the guard was not even armed! He was joined to a group of European deportees, and escorted slowly to the border. Days later he crossed the barbed wire barricade into freedom, doubtless one of the few people there to wish himself back in West China. At the time it all seemed hard to accept, let alone understand, but soon we realized that God had ordained it for our good in every way.

Chinese kitchen showing the usual type of stove.

Chinese bed like the one on which we sat as we ate the White Flower Street meal described.

LEFT TO RIGHT: *Our coolie, Mrs. Thunder's daughter, the first cook we had, the cook's little girl, and Mrs. Thunder.*

A group of Christians at Cloud Gate Place, our first outstation.

合川青年路福音堂全體同道歡送王傳福圖涵正先生攝影紀念 一九五0年 六月廿八日

Our church in Hochwan.

LEFT TO RIGHT: *Gordon, Luella, Dorothy, James, Don, Ruth, and Christine.*

A typical meat market.

Don and Ho Sz, our second cook.

Hochwan District Superintendent, Pastor Hsu, and Ed Knettler.

The Blossers coming out of China.

Interior view of the Hochwan Methodist Church which we used.

Evangelist John Chen and his wife, the two left in charge of the Hochwan church when the foreigners left.

Esther and Olin Stockwell, Methodist missionaries who helped in so many ways.

View of the border between Red China and Hong Kong, taken from the Hong Kong side. Final inspections are held at the right end of the bridge.

The McCammons, taken upon our arrival in San Francisco where Don met us. September, 1951.

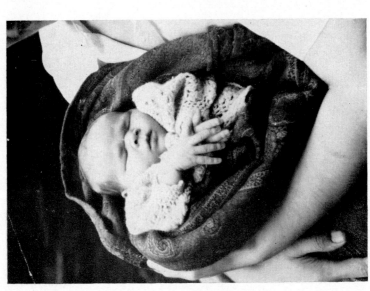

Julia E. McCammon, three days old, in Hochwan.

21. No Hiding Place

In the story of Don's arrest I mentioned the fact that at a public meeting of all Christians, our money was frozen, our goods sealed and then inventoried, and a general tightening-up began. An example of the tremendous fear this sort of publicity threw into the hearts of the Chinese makes me sad to relate. One member of our congregation was a very good friend of ours, a close neighbor, had been our language teacher for a number of months, and was our most dependable adviser in business matters and government relations. She knew everything there was to know about us and we trusted her completely. After the delegation leader read his statement concerning us that afternoon, she asked if she might say something. Permission was granted her; so she rose, looking very strange and doubtless feeling that way, and said something like this: "I just want to make it plain to everyone that I am not part of this group. I belonged to the Methodist Church here before the Mennonites came, and they never baptized me. I've never been too clear about who they are, where they came from, or why they came." It would have broken our hearts had we thought for a moment that this was her true feeling. No, I am sure that she was our friend as she stood there, and is today. This was just a frightened, desperate first reaction, exactly the sort of thing this meeting was designed to produce.

Our loyal pastor and his wife sort of lingered behind when folks left, and whispered that it probably would not be wise for them to come over any more. Next day was New Year's, and in the parade which ended up out at Don's trial there was a delegation of Christians including our co-workers waving a banner which declared that they were severing all connections with imperialistic foreigners. One thoughtful bit of preparation on their part had been to collect from us the week before their salaries for six months in advance. Believe me, we didn't begrudge it to them. Their lot at best was going to be very difficult.

Poor Pastor John just *thought* he wouldn't be visiting us! From that day on the government elected him to be our chief scribe in the many papers that were continually required. They gave him a rough time at every opportunity, not the least of their hecklings being untiring criticism of his handwriting! His patience and forgiving spirit through it all was enough to give them food for thought. It even fell to him to do the inventory—the government guards and inspectors merely sat around watching, listening to records, and smoking while we all worked! And to top off their troubles, John's wife came down with appendicitis during the parade, was carried home, and needed an operation immediately. So far as we were concerned, that was good! Here's why.

In the unpleasant indictment the important comrade had read, he stressed over and over the fact that we were dishonest. We searched our consciences and could only come up with one possible incident which anyone could question. So we determined to "confess" it, just to keep the air perfectly clear. But Don was gone, and we wanted him as far gone as possible before we threw any new monkey wrenches into the machinery. Now the logical time to raise this incident would be when we presented the finished inventory; so every day that our clerk couldn't come gave Don one more day's head start, should they care to make something of our confession. It really begins to sound like something, doesn't it? Here it is, in skeleton form.

When we were preparing to weather the turnover, we laid in all sorts of commodities which might come in handy when the present money was worthless. This included wheat, rice, corn; gold bars, silver dollars, and greenbacks. As time wore on we converted some of these to the new currency, but so far as we knew no provision was announced for the legal cashing of silver dollars. One of the early times when we thought we were leaving China, I asked our Chinese business adviser what we should do with those silver dollars. She practically fainted away at my words! We weren't supposed to have them, she said. Mr. Li, a friend of hers, recently was named as a possible holder of silver dollars and the searching party even tore up his shop floor boards in the hunt. Our trunks had already been searched a number of times, but no one had ever noticed those $96. Now what to do? In a couple of days this friend whispered that she knew someone who would take them, but that was black market and we weren't interested. Even to give them away would be contributing to someone's delinquency. So we pondered. Christine thought she could manage to stumble in the dark near an uncovered well and drop them in, but we had been told that we were followed everywhere, and the splash would rouse suspicion. On three sides of our compound were buildings higher than our walls, filled with young watching comrades day and night; so burial was out of the question. Which reminds me of the friends in the north who were ordered to kill their dog, then made to unearth his remains to prove that they hadn't buried something else instead.

Don thought of a public toilet, which is merely a pit that is never completely emptied, but again there was the splash. Ninety-six silver dollars make a heavy little bundle! The logical thing, of course, was to go to the bank, tell them we hadn't known about the turn-in date, and ask what to do. But we were in trouble already, and felt that our new supervisors were just looking for incidents to enlarge on. The unfortunate part was that this friend knew we had them, and wouldn't rest till she knew what we did with them.

Finally after a lot of silly talk and ridiculous ideas we all agreed that if Don put them someplace where we couldn't possibly get at them, we could say in good conscience that we didn't have any. So he climbed up one night and dropped them down the hole in the wall where our heating stove chimney left the room. A few months later when we were required to register all our money we didn't list them. But that woman knew we had them. Hence later, when the term "dishonest" was shouted at us, we thought of those wretched "big heads," as they were called, and determined to tell somebody about them. Which circuitous route brings us back to my joy at John's wife's appendectomy!

John went with her to the hospital and was slow getting back. And the inventory was endless, it seemed. But finally the day came to present our finished lists, "chopped" with our personal and mission seals to certify that they were complete and accurate. As so frequently happened, the authorities arranged for the meeting to take place on Sunday, thus inconveniencing us a bit more. Half a dozen officials came to receive them, and as we sat around discussing things, the leader asked me if I had anything to say. I said I did, and proceeded to tell this story, ending up by pointing at the pipe outlet on the wall. The comrades questioned me a bit, smiled as I had in the attempt to convince them that it was a funny story, said *use*, not possession was illegal (!), agreed that they should not be registered, accepted our lists, and walked away muttering one of the favorite phrases in their revised vocabularies, *hen t'an bei, hen t'an bei*—"How honest, how honest!"

22. Attempted Murder

Do you like dog stories? I guarantee that you won't like this one! We didn't either, but it had to be.

Don had a nice little red dog named Tinker, one "s" short from his real description, for he did "tink." They went everywhere together; he ate about as well as Don did, and did not in general lead a China dog's life. Don often had said that when the time came to leave he would kill him rather than let him be thin and mangy and ill-treated as most dogs were. Another possible fate for Tinker would have been the meat counter—he was fat and dog meat was sold publicly. But Don's time to leave came a bit unexpectedly, and there was no time to kill a dog, not even a little dog! When I visited Don in prison I told him we'd try, and it quickly became apparent that we would have to do something, for the constant stream of soldiers at the well and officials at the door were as irritated by Tink as he was by them.

The cook told me that we must get government permission to kill him. He heard that some soldiers saw a man sawing up his own table and took him to court. One could destroy nothing, though the soldiers themselves were catching stray dogs on the streets, putting a turn of rope around their necks, and pulling. So, law-abiding soul that I am, I trudged to the city police headquarters and asked (imagine!) if we might have permission, please, to kill a little dog.

The soldiers gave me a going over for being so stingy that I wouldn't feed it, but said to go ahead. We asked the old shoemaker coolie who did odd jobs for us, but he thought this job was a little too odd. Then we asked the soldiers who came daily for water if they'd shoot him, but they didn't dare waste a bullet. So we three ladies faced it—it was up to us! I simply couldn't, and they knew it. Christine liked Tinker a lot, and she said it would be too much like hitting Don on the head. Poor Ruth was elected—she liked Don as much as Christine did, I'm sure, but she had no great affection for Tinker, nor he for her. In fact, when the stage was set and she and Tinker and the blunt instrument were all in the same room, he wouldn't sit down. I had to go in and sit there to reassure him, hypocrite that I was.

Don had always said that one sharp blow would do it quickly, but I guess his blows and Ruth's didn't compare. At any rate, after that one blow was delivered I dashed from the room midst loud yelping, never looking back. Our Mrs. Thunder stood outside crying, and I paced and waited. After what seemed ages, Ruth emerged, looking completely wild. Just before this she had washed her hair and it was drying and flying in all directions. She was semi-hysterical, poor thing, and she screamed through her tears that the dog wouldn't die!

Christine had already taken refuge at the China Inland Mission, and I ran there now to tell them they *had* to help. Irmtrud, the German nurse, saw her duty and prepared to do it. She assumed that Tinker was unconscious, I guess, for she calmly unearthed some ether and a mask for him! She came back an aeon or two later to say that she couldn't go near Tinker, but *Ruth* needed company. So we all trailed back over and sat in the yard, trying to imagine how to deal with this tiny tyrant who had taken over the house. Finally Christine summoned enough courage to peer in the window, and Tinker smiled at her with his tail. She went in, and he jumped on her lap. A closer look at his head revealed that the skin was only slightly nicked in one place; so she washed off the blood and called me. He kissed me in the face, and I almost kissed him back. I promised him he could live—I had, after all, only promised Don that we would *try* to kill him. Mrs. Thunder gladly set out in search of the old lady from whom we'd bought Tinker, and soon came back with her. When she finally understood that we didn't want money for him, she was overjoyed to have him back. He remembered her and walked happily down the street without a backward glance. He knew Don was gone, and I fear he was only too glad to escape from such treacherous women. I called on Tinker several times, and always found him literally sharing the old grandmother's bed and board. I finally quit going because it made me too homesick for Don!

23. Open House

The last six months we were in Hochwan I learned new appreciation for the problems of the gold fish. From the day Don left until the day we left, we were under constant observation from uninvited guests. Our own friends didn't dare even to recognize us when we met on the streets, let alone come to our home. But we didn't lack for company.

We had a well on our property; so whenever there was water in it, people were there. Mostly it was a line of prisoners, under guard, carrying water to be used in the construction of buildings near by. They usually spent long rest periods in our easy chairs, since neither the carriers nor the guards were very eager to get to work. Many neighbors who had formerly bought water or carried it from public wells now followed the army's example and helped themselves to ours. In fact, when we once in a while shut the front gate for a few minutes, they would hammer on it and demand entrance. No "please" or "thank you" any more.

This new era also presented a marvelous opportunity for all the curious who had previously found no legitimate excuse to visit us. Now they came any time and all the time to roam over our yard, pick the flowers, observe our technique of doing things, and ask the same questions endlessly. "Is that soap you're washing dishes with?" "Is your food like our food?" "Aren't there any men here?" "Which is better, China or America?" "Why don't you go home?" "Is this a stove?" "Do you give medicine?" But these were mostly harmless country folk or neighbors, and we didn't worry too much about them.

A more difficult group to meet satisfactorily was the young soldiers themselves, who more often than not came looking for trouble. They wanted to get on the subject of Christianity, but only to argue. And they had a number of points in which they had been carefully schooled: Wall Street, Korea, the race problem, which they always wanted to discuss. It was so tiresome, for all they knew was the bit they'd been told and I, for one, found it hard to keep still when they glibly told us about families in Washington, D.C., living in caves, and Midwestern farmers not having enough to eat. They inevitably asked what we thought of the new government, and we always said it had its good points. What were they? We named some. Then, "What are its weak points?" And again we had to tread softly to keep our feet out of our mouths.

We did have some pleasant surprises in our early liberation days. Some of the boys and girls weren't really well enough indoctrinated to be turned loose, I fear. One lad whom we'd known in another city got assigned to Hochwan, and promptly came to see us on a friendly call. He loved music, and brought a number of other boys who loved it too. Do you know about the man who on Friday dutifully asked in the restaurant for whale, then shark, and finally had to settle for ham and eggs? These boys reminded me of that story. After first asking whether we had any Russian music, they hungrily pulled out the whole recorded *Messiah* and listened for a long time. The next day they came back, asked to borrow it, and played it to their whole outfit! That *Messiah*, by the way, was sold to the Chungking radio station and on the first Communist Christmas (they hadn't been there a month yet) was played in its entirety over the air!

The only occasions on which I was physically afraid of the Communists were the visits from a teen-age soldier who was mentally unbalanced. When he came with his buddies, they always took him home again, but when he came alone, we were in a difficult position. He carried a gun with bayonet, taller than he was, and flourished it with gusto as he ordered me to accompany him to this or that office. His hatred of me was so intense and his behavior so unpredictable that when I saw him coming I just stayed in my locked bedroom. I would have reported him, but the Communist soldiers wore no identifying badges or numbers or insignia of any kind. A colored silk tassel tied to the gun indicated an officer, but that was the extent of rank indication.

The city government was organized from the top down, finally arriving at neighborhood units. A sharp-tongued young woman from across the street, Mrs. Nail, was the head of our local unit, and she gloried in her new-found authority. She was forever dropping in with a group of friends, asking to inspect our residence book, professing great surprise to see Don's name struck off the list, and asking where he now was. One day in a short temper I answered, "You ought to know; you sent him." But usually I managed a more civil reply. The servants left soon after Don did, and there were but three of us left, yet Mrs. Nail made quite a ceremony of calling us all out, reading our names, and asking which was which!

Long before, I had promised our woman servant, Mrs. Thunder, my sewing machine when I left. Now she went first; so I asked permission to give it to her. Not only an emphatic "no" was forthcoming, but from then on Mrs. Nail called still oftener, with still more friends, and invariably she innocently asked them if they wouldn't like to see our "sewing room." Then she would rush in to see if the machine was still there.

A special source of amusement to us was the frequent visit of the "Cleanliness Committee." Again it was our neighbors, some mere children, and all from open, dusty homes which made ours look like a shining Betty Crocker kitchen in comparison. Christine, our dietitian, suffered the most from these calls, I think. Imagine the grace it took for her, trained as she was in sterile technique, to listen patiently to a lecture on how to scald the wooden chopping board. This from a little man whose dirt floor and cobweb-covered room we had seen ourselves! But she listened politely, bless her heart. The best one of all was the day she had been resting and reading on her bed, and left a book or two lying there when she went to meet this committee. They admonished her soberly that it was very unsanitary to have a book on a bed.

The prizetakers in this whole heckling war of nerves were the guests we entertained *daily*, without exception, the whole month of April. May Day was a great holiday, and every neighborhood must send a marching group for the parade. A couple of soldiers were assigned to each district to teach the men, women, and children to march. Each person had a small bamboo drum which he hit with sticks. The leader had cymbals which crashed out signals, and alongside (alongside our bedrooms, usually) sat a couple of noisemakers with large tom-tom sort of drums, taken from the temples. Believe me, a few days would have been tiresome, but a month was nigh onto unbearable. I can still dream ♩♩♪♪♩ ♪♪♪♪♪♪♩ without any effort! Not only would perhaps two groups be practicing at the same time, but the gates were wide open and half the town was crowding in to watch. Our house was a simple structure, one story high, and a room apiece; so there was no getting away. We streamlined the process to something like this: The three of us took turns, a day each, when we had to be polite. (I know Peter says, "Be hospitable to each other without secretly wishing you hadn't got to be!" But I'm being honest.) The other two took things to do and went over to the CIM to a back balcony where one could lock the door. The person who was being polite stayed home. When he heard the avalanche descending, he locked all the doors, including the toilets, and sat down in the breezeway. He *didn't* correct people for breaking the trees, tearing out the flowers, peering in the windows, breaking the chairs, spitting everywhere, or toileting their children on the sidewalk. He *did* get matches for those who asked, answer innumerable questions, provide drinks for the thirsty, and try to keep the children from breaking their necks in the little trees or falling down the well. When mealtime came the other two came home, we took a hammer and tacks and hung bed sheets over the windows, and proceeded to eat in "peace." When we all felt good at once we didn't hang the sheet, but it is hard to eat with faces everywhere and questions being shouted. It sounds pretty unsociable, but actually we were tense already and just couldn't take solid days of this. Anyway, if we'd all stayed and all turned on our charm at once, the drillmaster might never have taught his old ladies which were their left feet!

Then there were the borrowers. These were usually either high-school students or the dramatics group from the army. They never asked *us*, of course, for anything. They told our neighborhood chief what they wanted, and she decided whether we would loan it or not. They gave *her* the receipt for the goods, and usually returned them to her. We imagined that often Don, at least, was being featured in their productions, for they were very specific in their requests. "Mr. Ma's blue striped overalls, his tan pants and green shirt, and his brown suit this time." Other times it was just dress up for parades, with frequent calls for "eight white blouses and flowered skirts." They were sore grieved at our big feet. Ruth's were the only borrowable shoes!

Our yard soon came to be a favorite gathering place for neighborhood official meetings. The town crier would walk past, striking his gong and announcing a meeting of our district, and that night at dusk the representatives from all the homes in our area would surge in the gate. Each person carries a tiny bamboo stool to all such meetings; so they can just sit down anywhere and go into session. Mrs. Nail chaired these meetings, and it was a novel sight in China to see a woman so feared by the menfolk. She was always surrounded by a handful of men and ordered them about very freely. "A cigarette," she would say to no one in particular, and out the gate dashed someone to buy her one. (Just one, not a pack.) "A match," and another citizen had an opportunity to stay on her good side. It was hot weather and we liked to sit out in the evening in case a breeze came along. It should have been somewhat embarrassing to us when she started the meeting off with the question, "Who are our enemies?" No answer. Again the question, with a flash of her eyes that said she wanted an answer. "The Americans," they all shouted. When it got dark she sent a lackey to ask us for a lamp. The first time we were cheap enough to fix up a Chinese vegetable-oil lamp such as they would have had anywhere else, but she called us on that one and sent back for a "foreign-oil" or kerosene lamp. We were pretty disgusted, but just enough scared of her to comply.

The last week before we left, the long-awaited land reform came to our province. Before that two extended series of meetings were necessary. First came the "old heads" from northern provinces to teach the local leaders. Then the local leaders met with the country representatives to instruct them. Again our hospitality was tried to the breaking point! These boys got up early, and just at dawn would come a loud pounding on the gate. If we tried to ignore it they hied themselves to the upstairs of the house just over our wall, and from there they could practically lean in our bedrooms and shout! So it was hurriedly tack up heavier curtains, open the gate, and lock ourselves in our rooms. I might well still be in China as a result of one of those meetings. The country boys came earlier than the government men, and they insisted on coming in. Then until the leaders came they would amuse themselves by trying to see in our bedroom windows. One morning when I felt that the night was about half over, they came boisterously in and clustered around my window. I had double-thickness curtains up, but had left a tiny space high up for a breath of air to come in. One taller enterprising lad decided that if he jumped high enough he might see in; so he tried. I called to him to please go away, that this was a lady's bedroom. At this he laughed merrily, repeating to the seventy-five or so other farm boys that "She says please go away, it's a lady's bedroom." And he jumped harder than ever. That was too much for me that morning. He didn't realize it then, but he soon learned that I was just about six inches from him on the other side of the screen, preparing to brush my teeth. In a weak moment I dedicated my glass of water to another cause, and the next instant my friend was the spluttering laughingstock of his buddies. They simply hooted at him. The moment I let go of it I was afraid of the consequences, but I must admit that for a very short season the pleasures of sin felt good! The Chinese man on the street has a way of quickly judging who is guilty in such public clashes, and the boy was obviously found in the wrong. I was luckier than I dared hope. There were no uniforms there, and evidently the boys never reported the incident, for it was never mentioned again. What a major affair they could have made of it!

One session after another met all day long. The days were so hot that we simply could not remain in our stifling rooms; so we often joined the meetings in the only shady spots on our compound. It was very disconcerting for the leaders, partly because they didn't care to have us listening and partly because the delegates were much more interested in us and our magazines than in the tiresome repetitions of the lecture at hand. It must have been discouraging for everyone. I remember one day having heard a comrade laboring one point for half an hour. When he finished he asked, "Do you all understand?" Everyone nodded. "Then," said the leader, "suppose this comrade tell us what it means." "I don't know," said the farmer boy miserably. So it started all over again.

The evening session started off with a couple of lectures by local leaders who were trying desperately to repeat what had been hammered at them all day. Were I to give you a sample of what went on, you would find it hard to believe that dozens of grown men could sit with straight faces and listen to such infinite rehashing of the same few thoughts. Then they broke up into small groups to consider and evaluate what had been said in the large groups. This we endured, but when the chairman called for the little groups to come together again and bring their findings to the big group we rebelled. We told him it was bedtime for everybody, and we couldn't turn in till they were turned out. So with much bowing and smiling they filed by us into the night, doubtless as relieved to go as we were to have them leave. "We've troubled you, we've troubled you," they apologized. "No, no, not at all. Walk slowly," we answered, barring the gate after the last one and relaxing for a few short hours.

24. "Labor Is Glory"

If any of you have heard us talk at all, you've likely heard us relate the story of Christine looking in the soup kettle, and being startled by a full-front grin from a set of pig's teeth simmering therein. That was the same day we found the kitchen floor covered with cold greasy dishwater. The coolie was going to mop the floor and was soaking it first. Or maybe you read one of our letters which told how we were short on pans the summer we studied on the mountain; so the cook made the frosting for Don's birthday cake in his own private washbasin! Perhaps it sounds luxurious and maybe even wasteful or wrong to some of you when we speak of having servants, but they truly were a necessity if we were to have time for anything but housework. And, as a missionary friend from India said recently to me, "I refuse to call what I put up with 'luxuries'!"

When there were five and six of us living together, we had three servants at first, a cook, a woman, and a coolie. Later on we dispensed with the coolie. The cook was the hardest-working and the highest paid. He got about the equivalent of U.S. $5 a month. His work consisted of doing all the shopping, preparing all the meals and serving them, washing dishes, keeping the kitchen clean, washing the dish towels and his aprons, and all food extras like canning, refining sugar, rendering lard, and grinding grain. He also carried water from our well, ran it through the crock of sand, charcoal, and stones to clean it, and saw that we had cold boiled water on hand for drinking. Both cooks we had were good—the second one we had longer and he was a gem. It was almost impossible to ruffle his disposition! Both of them had worked for foreigners before; so we didn't have the job of starting from the very beginning. Ho Sz, our favorite and last cook, was very much relieved that we took turns planning meals. He told me that his last employer "perhaps not so much as once" told him what to make for a meal, and he lost a lot of sleep every night trying to think what to prepare. Whoever was in charge each week would consult with him each evening, for he shopped very early in the morning. Only a few blocks from our house was a large market where early each morning the choice vegetables, eggs, pork or goat, live chickens (with black skins), or live fish could be found. We got beef only a part of one month, and that was tough old water buffalo. Ho Sz had his favorite salesmen, of course, where he could buy for a little less and charge us a little more. "Squeezing" is an accepted practice in China. The servant who buys knows that he can get it for less than the foreigner could; so he boosts the price when reckoning accounts and pockets the difference. Everybody knows it and eventually assumes it as part of the cook's pay. We knew of only one servant in China who didn't "squeeze." The German women's cook was *perfectly* honest. Ten per cent was the average figure; if prices seemed unreasonable we had only to be seen out buying a few things ourselves and prices would quickly level off again! One didn't speak directly of it, but the word got around, the result was the same, with no feelings hurt and no "face" lost. Occasionally we really had to crack down. Our first cook was a cheerful liar. One day we asked him to buy about thirty *jin* (a *jin* is a bit more than a pound) of pork to can. When he came with it we asked how much it weighed. "Thirty-four *jin*." Then we horrified him by getting out a scale and weighing it. "Twenty-six *jin*." "My," said he, never batting an eye, "that strong wind must have evaporated a lot of it away on the trip home." (Three blocks!)

A funny thing—whenever we gave him a new recipe Ho Sz would never write it down till later. But he always had it right. Perhaps he had acquired his good memory before he learned to write. In doing accounts, too, he never hesitated over a figure, though he might have purchased a dozen items and was changing the actual price paid as he went along.

Ho Sz always went to church with us, and shortly before he left us he became a Christian. His final act toward us was a good evidence of a genuine conversion, we felt. After Don was deported the outside pressure on the servants was too great, and they were willing to go. We had wanted to dismiss them for months, since we were idle at home, but such matters were difficult until the servants were willing. Heretofore they had not been, knowing full well they'd not find another job as good.

Now, though, they were ready. The routine procedure for anyone leaving a job called for him to go through a government bureau and get a paper there which would help him prove his cleared status when he applied for his next job. Ho Sz refused to go, saying, "If I go there they'll ask me how much dismissal pay I asked you for. Whatever I say, it won't be enough to suit them and they'll make me ask for more. I know your finances are very uncertain, and I don't want to take more than I really need. I'll go without the paper. The Lord will look after me." That was more than just friendship; that was faith!

Our woman, whose name meant Mrs. Thunder, quite looked the part until she became a Christian. She had never been a servant before; in fact, had had servants herself; so it was a difficult adjustment. Her husband had two wives and she couldn't endure it; so she hunted a job. She was faithful in her work but glum and sour-looking, very rough to her little girl and unresponsive to us. When she accepted Christ her life made perfect material to show the changes He can make. She got a new philosophy about the dignity of labor, took pride in her work, learned to laugh, made friends with the women in the church, and was truly a "new creature." One of the loveliest sights one could see was to slip out in the evening and stand by her living room door. She and her daughter would be sitting in the dim light, their lamp sometimes only a cup of vegetable oil with a few pithy weed-heart wicks floating in it, singing a chorus or hymn. The girl went to school and could read; so she would teach her mother. Then they would pray together, for the little girl was a Christian, too. Later on Mrs. Thunder decided she must learn to read her Bible; so James taught her in literary class.

Her household tasks and church activities kept her busy and happy. We took turns helping her with the washing. A hand wringer was the extent of our modern equipment; so there was a lot of scrubbing to do. She ironed, beautifully, with flat irons. (The first time she dampened clothes we heard a loud spluttering and found her with a mouthful of water, spewing very evenly!) Cleaning she endured, and mending she enjoyed, especially after she learned to use the sewing machine. The only real thorn in her flesh was disposing of the "night soil." There were no flush toilets in our area. Human excrement was saved and sold to farmers who came in daily after it. They called loudly in the streets; whoever had a crockful opened the gates and called them in, and the bargaining began. The farmer paid the prices agreed, ladled it into his two shoulder buckets, and took it uncovered through the streets and home. Every field in the country has a lime-lined pit where night soil is accumulated until the crop then in season needs fertilizing. Then each separate plant receives a dipperful. For this reason we could never safely eat raw vegetables unless we had grown them ourselves.

The thing she enjoyed most was preparing Chinese food. In the wintertime we ate one meal a day of Chinese food, and Ho Sz wasn't much good at it. We didn't want to hurt his feelings, but whenever we dared we asked her to cook for us, and we all ate together. She had a number of specialties of which we never tired. Just before she left us she recalled one famous dinner she'd never fed us; so we had it. A tiny charcoal fire sat in the middle of the table, and on it boiled a delicious kettle of soup with plenty of red pepper in it. When the soup had boiled sufficiently, she quickly dumped in tiny chips of pork, fish, bean curd, cabbage, green onions, spinach, pea vine tips, and whatever else was on the market. It cooked a very few minutes more, and we consumed vast quantities with rice. It doubtless tasted more exciting than it sounds. It was simply delicious.

Mrs. Thunder didn't know where her living was coming from, hence wasn't quite as considerate of us in her final accounting as Ho Sz had been. But we parted friends, and she made a millionaire's exit—in fact, she was one! She still couldn't bear to admit her new status in life, so went to her relatives literally weighed down with expensive gifts, all the way from live chickens carried by little bamboo strings, to her famous cured fish-heads, tails, innards, and all.

Just before I left Chungking she came to see me there. She just had to risk it to see our new baby! She told me that her daughter was in a former church school, where now there was not one professing Christian. Mrs. Thunder herself knew no Christians. She lived with her relatives, and they forbade her to read her Bible, lest neighborhood officials drop in unexpectedly and see it. So she was completely alone with her newfound faith. That is the last we know of Mrs. Thunder.

❖ ❖ ❖

The day the servants left, we three had a family parley and divided up the work. From then on we had no time to be bored. What would we have done without each other! As it was, we really had fun lots of times, and kept busy. Poor Ruth complained that she had no pin money—Christine could "squeeze" on the marketing and I had the income from the night soil but where was she to get her spending money?

My income was a questionable blessing. It took a while to learn to enjoy opening the main gate and roaring at a prospective buyer, then haggling with him over the price of my merchandise. At first I tried several times to agree with some friendly country boy to come regularly and get it for nothing (the price only amounted to a penny or two). But immediately they became suspicious of anything free; so to the end I had to drive a daily bargain!

Christine was a careful shopper and we ended up by eating better for less. To conserve fuel we cooked on the living-room heating stove except on baking and ironing day. It took some practice to gauge the heat when the bed of coals was several feet away from the top of the stove, but the results were excellent. When the bread got low, Christine would pour some concoction into a pint bottle and set it in a pan—presto, we had Boston brown bread, or steamed pudding, or perhaps a nameless invention.

Ruth rose with the chickens and the neighbors to scrub the floors before we wanted to walk on them. More than once she almost broke up solemn meetings on our premises by popping out of her room in a bright-colored dress, singing some gay tune, and proceeding to shake the scatter rugs and dust mop vigorously in all directions. The boys from the country had never seen the like! Often as our soldier-neighbors leaned over the compound wall and watched us working, they would grin and shout in English a translation of one of the phrases used to spur them on, "Labor Is Glory!"

Christine was justly proud of her pioneering work in the kitchen. Keeping yeast alive with potatoes, baking bread, rendering lard—these things weren't so unusual. But to see a huge batch of sugar through the refining process and have it come out clean, dry, and fluffy—that was something of an achievement. When we bought sugar it was wet, coarse, dark brown, and full of impurities. First she brought it to a boil, with plenty of water and lots of old egg shells, sometimes a whole egg and a little milk added. Next it was strained through a clean cloth where a frightful collection of sticks and stones remained. Then back onto the stove for a long process of slow boiling and continual skimming. At just the crucial hair-spinning ball-forming stage we would whisk it to the back court where we took turns holding the pan and beating the cooling sugar. As it cooled it crystallized of course, and suddenly one knew whether it was right that day or not. Perhaps it was in hard dry lumps, which meant it must be crushed or sifted before using. Rarely it was cool and not yet dry, which meant, alas, that it hadn't cooked long enough. But usually it was just right, and that's more than we could say for poor Ho Sz's sugar. He seldom had the patience to cook it long enough; then would blame the sugar!

One major experiment remains an unfinished story, for we left before it was ready. We had a really promising batch of vinegar brewing, concocted mostly from vague memories of watching the cook. Chinese wine, native yeast, sugar, rain water—I forget what all went in. I have a notion that whoever eventually inherited it rejoiced, and likely consumed it in larger quantities than we would consider temperate.

After we had lived in Hochwan for several months, we persuaded a friend who owned a herd of dairy cattle in Chung-king to "carry" a few to Hochwan. From then until we left we had wonderful fresh milk daily, from (tell it not!) cows with imperialistic backgrounds.

Fresh fruits helped us immensely in varying the diet. Cherries, apricots, peaches, bananas, persimmons, plums; all these and more found their way to our door, for our fondness for fruit was known abroad. We canned a lot, for all but the citrus fruits were in very short seasons. Szechwan tangerines were so good that we seldom bothered to peel the oranges, which were still better. Both of them went on for months! Oranges and eggs, which we usually buy by the dozen, are sold by tens in China. Spices were purchased at one shop but taken to another to be ground. Cuts of meat were unique, to put it mildly. Since the Chinese always cube their meat in preparing it, the grain doesn't matter to them. We had some wild experiences in trying to get what we wanted, and seldom succeeded. One day after Ruth and I had been responsible for company dinner on Sunday, I wrote home:

"Our dinner was built around a rolled roast, which is a story in itself. You would have to see it to believe the pieces of meat we get. I asked Thali's cook to buy a piece which we could roast and slice cold. I even showed him from where on my own back, but he came back with a long, flat, wrong-grained slab with bones full length down the middle. We stood and held it and groaned after he'd gone. By the time we got it in shape to roast, Ruth and I felt we were ready to qualify for a certificate in advanced surgery. We used about half of Christine's ball of string!"

Grinding was fun but tiresome. We had a heavy locally made stone mill, one stone on another, with a bamboo handle on the top stone by which we turned it horizontally. Into a small hole on the top stone we dropped the wheat or corn, a few grains at a time, and the cracked wheat or flour or corn meal came out in proportionate fineness to the amount we put in at one time.

Here's an indication of the state my brain was in when I finally reached America. A friend had taken me to her fruit room to show me something and stopped beside some glass jars of corn meal. "Do you like home-ground corn meal?" she asked, "Charles grinds it himself so we'll be sure it's perfectly clean."

"Home-ground corn meal!" I exclaimed, "I don't believe I ever heard of it before."

I'd been home an hour before the idiocy of the remark struck me! I'm sure I've ground a lot more corn meal in my day than Charles has!

25. All Things Come ...

About a month after Don left, we were summoned to police headquarters. "Is it true that you want to leave China?" we were asked. We admitted the fact, thinking about the file folders they had on us, full of applications, twenty-five to thirty pictures of each of us, references, histories, and every other imaginable type of data, and wondering why they needed to ask! We were told to prepare individual letters giving the reasons why we wanted to leave, and they would "think about it." This had to be carefully done, with more emphasis on health reasons, our home church's recalling us, and the strength of the church in New China, rather than the obvious facts that we were a menace to our friends and of less than no value to the work because of the efficient and deadly propaganda of the new regime. Another month passed and we were sent for again, this time to be told that we might make application. Not as though we hadn't already made application eight months ago, but we gratefully seized the blanks and went home. A new wrinkle in this application was that we were to tell the date by which we would be out of the country, and to attach a detailed list of everything we would take. Both were well-nigh impossible, since the second depended on the first, and the first was totally up to them, not us!

Then came weeks of no reply. The date we had suggested for crossing the border came and went and we had not yet crossed the threshold. Friends in Chungking strongly recommended that I ask permission to go there for our prospective baby's arrival, since the local doctors would hardly dare to help; so I did apply. There were two doctors in our town whom I would have trusted. Both had studied some western medicine and both were friends of ours. The first, a Christian, merely said, "Oh, you can do it yourself," when I asked if he might help. When I asked the second whether he would help if I couldn't go to Chungking, he replied, "Surely they will let you." "But if they don't?" I tried to pin him down. "Surely they will," he repeated, and I knew that was as close as they could come to saying no. They both were sorry, and I knew it.

It was in making this application that I did the first smart thing in all of our negotiations, and that wasn't intentional. When they asked whether I wanted to go to Chungking to stay I said no, only till the baby came, and then back to Hochwan again. Since their aim in life seems to be not to give the American what he wants, that was the right answer. When I finally was allowed to go, the only condition was that I could not come back! By then, coming back to Hochwan was the least of my desires.

On the application I asked to go a month before the baby's coming. That date passed and no word. I started going to ask, and was always told, "No word yet; we'll let you know." These excursions got less and less pleasant as the date came closer and the weather grew hotter. I stood on the street and talked into a head-level window to ask my questions; so wasn't too visible to the man in charge, but the truth of my condition was always attested to by a little friend who lived near the government office. She came out every time and stood at my side exclaiming in tones to be heard a block away, "What a *big* dress!" Expectant mothers in China just wear their dresses tighter and tighter and finally partly unbuttoned on the side; so a smock looked quite like a tent to them. Finally I was told not to come any more to ask about my permit. "We'll let you know." That was all we could do; so we "laid down our hearts," believing as a Chinese friend who wrote: "Pray God you can go Chungking, but if not, He will be responsibility."

Now began another and the worst chapter in this war of nerves. Word would come for the two CIM ladies and Ruth and Christine to come to headquarters. "Everybody but you," was the way the messenger put it, pointing to me. Action had started on their applications to leave the country, but no word on mine! In spite of having been told to stay home, I went once more for an interview and told the man in whose charge we were that I could hardly stay alone at such a time. He smiled unpleasantly and told me, as he had told the others, that if they said "go" the girls would go, and if they said "stay" I would stay. He suggested I get a Chinese friend to live with me, but he and I both knew that was out of the question. The girls were told off soundly for raising the subject each time; so once more we had to commit it to God, and trust Him to overrule.

One last attempt we made to find the holdup was to ask our "boss" if he had any suggestions how we might get rid of the extra money we had on hand. After weeks of writing we had caught up with the proceeds of our last large check. (The first two treasurers handling it were now in prison and it was hard to keep up with the books!) Instead of being destitute we now had too much money, if, as we had heard, we were going to be held till we spent it all! So we gave him a chance to indicate that they had use for it, but he didn't take the bait.

Months before we had almost stood on our heads to find "guarantors"—someone to vouch for our behavior and financial obligations, past, present, and future. When we each found the required one they had immediately required four more each, an impossibility, of course. Now when the other four ladies were asked to find guarantors again, we were actually relieved, for we knew they couldn't possibly find them, hence wouldn't be going off without me. But when they reported to the official that they couldn't find them, he told them the requirement would be waived!

At this point we all felt that I was clearly being discriminated against, and that a possible reason was Don's waiting in Hong Kong. He had been ordered to go home, but once in free territory had waited in the hope that we would soon be coming. Now we felt that perhaps I was going to be held till he left. To go home and face the public without me meant much more loss of "face" than to wait in Hong Kong, and face means much in China.

So I wrote a most difficult letter. I had been writing to Don in my poor longhand on purpose, knowing that one must be a long-time acquaintance to make head or tail of it. But this time I typed very clearly, something like this: "Why don't you go home and face the music? Take your medicine like a man. You've been wrong and now you must pay for it. Nobody will understand and it will be awful, but you should go." He caught on immediately and answered promptly in like vein. In just a few days we had clear telegrams and cables signed "Don McCammon" tracing his flight from Hong Kong to San Francisco to Omaha. It was truly a hard thing to ask of him, but not for the reasons they thought. We think to this day that it was the solution to the situation, though we can never know for sure.

The girls' next step was to advertise their intentions of leaving, thus giving any accusers a chance to even the score. Since we had no newspaper, the advertisement was simply written on blackboards here and there in the city and set in prominent places on the sidewalk. Once more, nobody came forward and there was nothing to stop their going.

We were all more sober than we had yet been, for the way out was certainly hidden from our view. Christine and Ruth were busy buying wood and having it chopped, having coolies haul in coal and kerosene, canning, and in every way helping me prepare for the eventuality of their being forced to leave. I think I can truthfully say that I was less upset than any of the rest. Leaving would have been more awful than being left. I was holding tight to the verse in I Corinthians which says, " . . . God can be trusted not to allow you to suffer any temptation beyond your powers of endurance. He will see to it that every temptation has a way out, so that it will never be impossible for you to bear it." We did everything we possibly could, even to phoning long distance in an attempt to find a safe way to make the baby come. But that failed too; so we waited to see what better thing God had planned. We weren't long in finding out!

Each step on the girls' papers took time, and I'm sure I've not listed them all. The first thing we knew July 9 was here, we girls were still together, and the baby's birthday party was under way. Three of the four girls were completely new at midwifery; this was my first baby, and the German nurse had witnessed only two deliveries and assisted at none. We still felt it would be a relief to have help; so once more asked the doctor to come. He stuck his head in the door just long enough to say, "It's nothing, nothing at all," and dashed out. But as the hours wore on and we wore out we were inclined to disagree. We thought it was something quite major, and something we didn't know too well how to cope with. We stopped in the midst of our activities and prayed to God for clear guidance. I'm not given to groaning during prayer, but I did that time! Then one of the girls ran to the church (where we'd not been for months) to talk to the evangelist (whom we'd not spoken to for months). She intended to ask him to go for a doctor, but he informed her that the entire medical profession of our city was holding a meeting in the church right there. By then the church was frequently used for such meetings, and this time it was providential. Included in such a meeting would be Chinese root-and-herb medicine doctors, my two friends, trained and self-trained midwives, and pure quacks. When the meeting was over John spoke to the chairman about our request. Whether it was curiosity or a matter of professional honor we will never know, but he gave his permission for someone to come. Evidently it was decided that there was safety in numbers, for a few minutes later not one or two or three, but an even dozen representatives filed silently into my 13′ x 15′ bedroom, already occupied by five people and considerable furniture. We actually had to ask a few of them to wait outside. Not much was said—a few suggestions were offered, such as: "shut your mouth," "shut your nose"— and nothing was done by any of them except the Christian doctor who laid his cool hand on my hot head and kept it there. When I thanked him afterward he said, "Did you like it? I did it for my wife when our baby came, and she thought it helped." The baby came safely, and a thrilling experience it was for us all. We all feel sure that had we needed help from the visitors that day it would have been forthcoming.

A couple of hours later we formulated a cable to the Board office in Elkhart, and Ruth sent it yet that night. That was Monday, and Wednesday noon we had Don's answering cable of rejoicing. It was weeks before we heard how he learned the good news. The Board had asked him to come to Elkhart from Omaha, where he was visiting his parents. The cable came after he had left Omaha; so the alert Board folk called Dorothy Bean, Ruth's Chicago sister, and told her what train Don was on. A few minutes later as he was sitting gloomily on one of the hard benches, waiting to board the Elkhart train, she rushed up and told him. Which just goes to show you that you never can be sure what people are talking about in the train station!

The next few days were absolutely packed. Christine had earlier felt bad about going home without completing a full term of service, but after that week she said she felt she had done the equivalent! In the first place, I needed medical attention beyond the ability of the girls; so the very doctors who had earlier refused now came. They went to our Mrs. Nail and had her send representatives along to look and listen, lest anyone suspect it was other than a professional call. There were two days of such activity. On the third day the little

government messenger came for "everybody but you" again.
Christine stayed with me and Ruth went with the CIM ladies
and our prayers. Her whoop of joy when she came home still
echoes in my ears. They had been handed their papers and
told to go tomorrow, then at the last minute had been told
that I could go as far as Chungking with them! That was all
we could ask, for there were dear friends in Chungking, willing
and able to care for tiny Julia and me. I would not be left
alone! It was a tremendous relief to us all. It was late afternoon when the permission was given, and Ruth persuaded the
official that we simply must have the next day to get ready.
Processing my moving papers, for instance, would require
hours of running from bureau to bureau for official "chops."
Finally he granted that day of grace. Ruth finished up a multitude of affairs outside, and Christine fought the battle of the
gate at home while packing for us both. Everyone was determined to walk right into my bedroom to see this foreign baby,
yang wa wa, as they called her. If she hadn't been so tired,
it would have been funny to see mild Christine actually lock
my door and stand with her back against it saying, "Excuse me
but our customs differ, and we have no such custom." A very
few friends who had heard we were going dared to come, and
of course they came in. But the perfect strangers with half
a dozen germy youngsters in tow had to go away disappointed.

My packing all had to be redone, for now I was only moving
to Chungking, not leaving China, with a baby instead of alone,
and for how long nobody knew. An official had earlier told me
I'd not get out that year; so I had to plan for cold winter,
though that was hot July. Curios? No. Nice clothes? No.
Everyday warm things? Yes, in a minimum. No time, no
space, no energy for inspections, no desire for any arguments
or questions.

The day a lot of localites had long looked for was here. Since
a year ago we had been warned that we may not sell or give
anything away. Now circumstances made it impractical to

take much with us. So? So we were told to find some person who would assume the responsibility for everything we left behind. Impossible, of course, and we packed on without even trying. Late in the afternoon came Mrs. Nail and entourage walking into my bedroom with a letter. "You must leave Hochwan tomorrow. The only condition is that you never come back. [Remember my request asking to come back?] Before you go you must find somebody to substitute in the management of your property until you come back. (!) If you are unable to find such a person, you might consult with your neighborhood government authorities."

"Do you understand?" asked Mrs. Nail. We did. "Do you have anything to say?" We did. "As spokesman for our group I politely ask you if you would be kind enough to help us in this not-easy situation. Would you accept this responsibility?" A hurried conference resulted in an affirmative response, thus placing on their already loaded shoulders a house, lot, complete clinic equipment and medicines, household furnishings, even including a set of Fostoria and a refrigerator, and the bulk of our personal goods. Oh, yes, and a sewing machine!

While Ruth and Christine toiled on, and Julie and I lay in bed and tried not to look amused, they came in like a swarm of ants. Everything left behind must be listed in detail. Contents of every drawer, every cupboard, *everything*, they listed. They were much too proud to imply that some things were strange to them, and the names they attached were really enlightening. An old scrap of pajama leg which I used for a dustcloth: "one flowered skirt." A little desk pad for 3 x 5 cards: "one typewriter." A punctured rubber tube: "hot water bottle." "You called that out earlier!" "That was a *cold* water bottle." So it went till 2:00 A.M. on the morning of our leaving. Maybe not just like a private room in a lying-in hospital, but certainly more entertaining!

At four we started getting ready, and soon the crowd began to gather. Christine locked me in again! Time to go, and the carriers wouldn't touch the trunks. Mrs. Nail had left word for them not to move till she came; so we sent for her. She said they had been copying lists since 2:00 A.M. but still weren't finished. "Lists for whom?" I asked. "One for you," she began, but I stopped that quickly by saying we didn't need any list, and were only grateful to them for bothering with all our things. "But," she said, "we need your chops on the lists." "Simple," said I, "here is the Mennonite seal, and here is my personal seal as the head of the family. Okay?" She nodded to the carriers and our trunks started for the riverside. Finally Christine decreed that I could come out. A chair for me was placed by my door, I got in, the crowd pressed close as Christine handed five-day-old Julie to me, and we were off. Many of the people to whom we would have said good-by were there, smiling quietly, and the rest were in inconspicuous places in the crowd that lined the road to the river. Some even dared to voice the lovely Chinese good-by, *yi lu ping an,* "One road of peace!" Julia was the first white baby ever born in Hochwan, and everybody wanted a look. I was proud to have them see her, for she was an uncommonly sweet little pink and gold bundle, I thought! She and I sat quietly for an hour on the dock while the boat waited for another complete inspection of all baggage. It had been done thoroughly the night before and locked, but these were the water police and that was different. All the while a semi-hysterical woman was pulling on Thali's dress and complaining to the soldiers that she owed her money. Thali refused to give her the few cents to quiet her, and I began to wonder again whether we would actually get off. Finally we were on the boat. Then came a woman who had worked for us a little, following me on the boat and demanding money. But when in a loud voice I rehearsed to her how many days she had worked for us and how much we had already overpaid her in an effort to keep out of trouble, the crowd started muttering at her and she left in a hurry. One last whistle and the line of water between us and the floating dock widened. Soon we were up on the top deck, Julie and I on a cot and the other four circled around us. The circle grew, and the questions began again; very natural questions for China. "Have you fulfilled your month?" (Chinese ladies never come out before a month after the birth of a child.) "Do you have enough milk?" "Aren't you afraid to come out without tying a rag around your head?" "How do you dare to eat cold things?" (We were consuming tomatoes and watermelon by then.) "Where is her father?" Then came a bright-eyed boy in uniform to break up the pleasantries. He began a loud discussion with Thali about Christianity and Communism. It finally came to a close when he said, "I suppose you claim that God created you?" Thali, who handled the language well, answered, "Yes, and I guess you came from a monkey?" The crowd roared good-naturedly and the boy retired to his seat.

We had several quiet hours then to ponder our emotions. We were near hysteria with joy and exhausted with relief to be all together, leaving no one behind. But we were immeasurably sad to be leaving what we had hoped would be our permanent home, and those we had so recently come to know and to love. We were almost angry that it was thus, yet we were profoundly grateful to God for His undertakings in our behalf. We were reminding ourselves that this was not our work, but the Lord's, and we were finding comfort in the sure knowledge that He is almighty. We didn't talk much that day, but I know that each in her heart was renewing her vow to count anything worth while if it could teach her, as this past week had, the peace of completely casting herself on the Lord's mercy. Through my own heart kept running this couplet from a hymn which Hannah had introduced me to, and which we had sung together:

"Jesus, I am resting, resting in the joy of what Thou art,
I am finding out the greatness of Thy loving heart."

14

26. ... To Him Who Waits

Pulling into Chungking was a real thrill, for it was another chance to show off the baby! Several from the house where I was to live were there at the riverside, and long before we docked I was leaning on the rail, holding Julia up to be admired. Soon we were off and a glad reunion it was—friends whom we'd not seen for more than a year, but who had been so faithful in their letters and their prayers. What a relief it was to have a man take over the baggage problems! In just a few minutes we were up the many steps by sedan chair, and being warmly welcomed into the Canadian Mission Home by George and Nell Rackham, our thoughtful host and hostess. More than coincidence was the fact that among the transient family there was an American doctor whose specialty was baby cases, and an English nurse who was longing for something to do. In a short time both Julie and I were tucked into clean sheets, thoroughly checked over, and completely at peace with the world.

Weary Ruth and Christine could forget their cares, too, and when they finally relaxed it was long hours before they were caught up on their rest. An upstairs room seemed so quiet and safe, the food tasted so good, the people were so kind—it was almost more than I could take. Esther lived there too. Olin had been imprisoned and she had been ordered to move out of their home. When she came in later to say good night we tried to pray together, but all we could do was weep. She had done everything she could to get permission to come to me, should I be left alone. I told her then and I still say that our arrival was more like going from hell to heaven than anything I had ever experienced. It was little enough in comparison to the suffering some had endured and are enduring, but it was not easy, and the relief was exhausting.

A story which waited us there stunned me. You read it in your papers before I knew it, likely. I have written here and there of Hannah Cole, our very good friend, who was on the same boat coming to China, was my study-partner in school, and whose friendship was one I much treasured. I was sure we would soon meet to show each other our new babies, since Coles were on their way out, too. But Chungking friends told us how God had gently taken Hannah home on the trip out, and that George and his four small children had only the week before flown through. The shock was terrific, yet I remembered her very last letter and its closing sentence, which had ended, "Even so, come, Lord Jesus." So He had come, for her, and if anybody ever had the right papers for heaven, Hannah did. Hers was a radiant life for Christ. Hers was a death I will not question. I can almost hear her beautiful soprano voice singing with the angel choirs, and I rejoice to know that she is truly "finding out the greatness of His loving heart."

A strange assortment of people we were in Chungking—different backgrounds, nationalities, and denominations, and each one delivered out of trying experiences by God's power. The second day after we arrived we came together in a service of thanksgiving and praise to God for His goodness to us. The whole group took part in reading, songs, and prayer. I doubt if a service ever could mean more to the participants than that one did. As I wrote to Don later, "to sing again with that many people, with hearts as full as mine was, was almost too much, but *not* to sing would have been worse; so I sang."

To be there was for us at least a step of "arriving," but not all who attended had attained even that step. One was just in town for the day, and had to go back to her trying situation, but she went strengthened. One was that far, but without loved ones; so her joy was far from full. One knew his Jordan was still to be crossed and these were days of spiritual preparation. It was an atmosphere which is most difficult to share with a weak pen—one had to be a part of it, only then could he truly share.

That same night soldiers came to announce that all but Chungking residents must move to Chinese inns to wait boats. Our family was abruptly cut from the teens to seven and the baby. From then on we entertained no more guests, and we really rattled in that huge house.

Ruth and Christine hated to go, but they went with my blessings. They had done everything possible, and I was in good hands. There was no place in China I would rather have been. They waited about a week in the inn, with restricted liberty so far as going out was concerned, but unrestricted liberty in chasing the thousands of bedbugs who slept with them. How thankful they were that the baby didn't need to be there! Then they were on a river boat to Hankow, fifth class, which meant squatter's rights on the open deck, day and night. They were in close company with some English girls and a young vice-consul whose only possession, a pillow, dropped overboard when he leaned forward the first few minutes out!

They had interesting conversations with girl soldiers going to Peking. In typical fashion, the young comrades wanted to catch them in talk about Christianity. One night late they were talking to Christine and one asked, "If Chairman Mao dies, will he go to hell?" To which she replied diplomatically, "I believe what the Bible says. Ho-hum, I'm sure sleepy. Goodnight." And she closed her eyes. Perhaps she was remembering a friend who had been detained several months for adding a line when he read publicly from Philippians 2:9-11. To "every knee should bow . . . and every tongue confess . . . " he added, "and that means Mao and Stalin, too!"

They went by train from Hankow to Canton and thence to the Hong Kong border. The main story I remember them telling from this lap of the trip was the uncertainty of ever knowing whose eye one would catch across from her when she woke up in the uncurtained hard upper berths. Sometimes men, sometimes women, some friends, some not, for the berths were hard boards and nobody could lie there very long. They got out safely while it was still July.

The Eugene Blossers had arrived in Hong Kong only a couple of days after Don in January. Theirs was quite an uneventful exodus, for it was from Chengtu where things were better handled, and early enough in leave-taking time that some troubles hadn't started yet. In fact, they had more trouble in Hong Kong! Eugene had a hard case of measles and Luella broke her arm.

Our Chungking family settled into a hot-weather routine. It was often over 100 degrees in our bedrooms, and it was there that we could be most cool. When the men went down in the morning, they stayed down, and the ladies stayed up, very informally. One lady soon got her pass to leave; so we were three preachers and three preachers' wives, but only one couple among us! Evenings were pleasant, when we often read aloud together, sang quartets, walked on the tennis court, tried our hand at badminton or tennis, or just watched the lights come on and the world go by.

The days of my wait in China were days of rich blessing. God made it abundantly worth while, both as He worked in my own life, and as He permitted me to see Himself at work in others. I won't embarrass my friends by mentioning names, but surely in those Chungking months I saw Christianity that worked. Thomas Kelly speaks of the heart being enlarged through suffering and I saw the agonizing process in the heart of a dear friend till my own almost broke. She who had more grief to bear than any of us could begin to know, she it was whose tender heart entered into our daily petty problems till we sometimes could hardly stand ourselves. One was lonely to talk of his family; so they talked; he was longing to pray with someone; so they prayed; he needed to pour out his troubles; so she listened. One was sick a lot; so she visited and discussed symptoms, encouraged, and cheered. One needed music; so she made it. A brilliant student wanted intellectual companionship; so she read his recommendations and challenged him with her grasp of them. I needed someone to share our dear baby; so she shared perfectly. I needed to laugh; so we laughed. I hadn't much feeling left, but I needed silent understanding and reassurance; it was there always. You know her. There aren't two of her in this book, or anywhere. I tried to write it once, this thankfulness, but could only end up crying,

> "Thanks to God that lives lived heavenward
> Are to earth such benedictions."

By that time there were guards at the gate who allowed few people in and none of us out except the servants to market and us to the foreign office when we were sent for. They frequently came in at night to call us all down and take roll, then search the house to see if any unregistered guests were there.

In a few weeks I became a Chungking resident, after a long stiff interview with the woman lawyer in charge of foreigners. She wanted all dates from kindergarten on, mission history, church history, Don's "criminal record," and my opinion about why I was detained. That was completely unanswerable—anything would have been wrong. Discriminated against? They wouldn't do that! Justly in need of punishment? For what? Had the wrong friends? Not so! So I hesitated, recalling that all the way to the office that morning I had sat far back in the ricksha, inconspicuous in dark glasses, murmuring to myself, "Thou wilt keep him in perfect peace whose mind is stayed on thee." And even as I hesitated, my interrogator was called out, stayed for three quarters of an hour, and upon her return had quite forgotten her train of thought. At the end of the interview she said gruffly, "That's all. Go home. Don't come out again until we send for you." Then, as I turned to go, in quite a different tone of voice she asked, "How much did your baby weigh?" I went home happy that behind her grim demeanor she still felt a woman's tenderness toward helpless new babes. Doubtless she reckoned that Julia was helpless in her choice of despicable imperialists for parents!

During the weeks of waiting that followed, we welcomed even the smallest deviations from daily routine. One day we all became excited when some government inspectors came to decide how much of the house they would occupy as of the next day! The moment they had gone our hostess turned a meaningful look on one family member, who promptly passed it on to another. I gathered that there was a story I hadn't heard, and soon I was piecing it together from their hasty actions.

An American friend from a distant city was imprisoned for months. One of the charges against him was that he had stolen valuable antique Mandarin jackets from the local museum. The fact was that he had been buying a lot of them from peddlers to take home. They were selling for very little, and really worth a lot. They made ideal gifts to Stateside friends. Some students had actually brought a big package of them as far as Chungking for him earlier, leaving them with someone in this house. The recipient was horrified to keep them, but had to because they were wrapped only in a cloth and doubtless the students had inspected the bundle. If they should report the incident, and this friend were to say he had destroyed them, alas, his would be an attitude of disrespect for Chinese art and beauty! On the other hand, if they were found there and acknowledged to be the real owner's property, then this friend would be harboring stolen goods. On the horns of the not-infrequently-confronted dilemma, friend one appealed to friend two to hide them well!

Now came the word that the government was moving in, hence the apprehensive looks floating around. It was the only questionable bundle in the house, somewhat like our silver-dollar story related earlier. The hostess meant business—they must go, and now. The holder meant business too—bring them on! The hider hustled off to do their bidding, and soon we were gazing at a whole armful of the most beautiful jackets imaginable, replete with exquisite handwork in gold thread. Museum pieces, every one of them. But there was no time for regret or sentiment. Out front went number one, ready to have a coughing fit should the gate guards note the smoking chimney on this scorching August day. Out back went a second, ostensibly walking the baby but actually determined to keep the servants from the living room at any price. Our hostess armed herself with a poker, two of us equipped ourselves with scissors, and the tragic destruction of beauty began. Snip, snip, through the padded places; rip, rip, through the rest. Add several crumpled pages of *Saturday Evening Post* to each strip to kindle it, and into the heating stove. Endless poking finally saw it into the ash pan, which number six emptied often down a wide crack in the side porch. In an hour the deed was done, the floor was covered with huge drops of perspiration, the baby was sleeping beautifully, several minds were relieved, and the stove was cooling. Next day came word that the new residents had decided not to come!

27. Destination: Don

At the close of my Chungking interview I had asked whether I might make application to leave the country. "You already have, twice," was the curt reply. But several weeks later came word that I should apply, if I'd like to go! I did, and in a short time received permission to advertise my intention of leaving in the newspaper. This was meant to bring forth troublemakers, but all it brought me was a very welcome visit from Mrs. Thunder and her daughter. I can't imagine what they told the guard at the gate to move him to let them come in. The most he was doing by then was accompanying anyone on legitimate business and listening to all that was said.

When it began to look as though I might really go, I started casting about for a way to dispose of my excess funds. Only the equivalent of a dollar or two could be taken across the border; more than that must either be remitted to someone in China or it was confiscated. I had a cool ten million too much, which amounted to U.S. $350. No more Mennonites; so there was nobody to remit to. Everybody else had been preparing for the unpredictable months ahead; so had enough cash on hand. I worked on the idea of buying something small and valuable, and selling it again when I got out. There was an interesting foreign girl who had a way with the guards. She had a Chinese husband, and had lived in Chungking for some years. She did everything she could for us, and we returned it whenever possible. I presented my problem to her, and she promptly suggested either a diamond ring or a pair of earrings. Her husband knew diamonds and I could trust him to get something which would sell for a lot more on the outside. She brought various samples for me to see, but I was apprehensive and hesitant because for all I knew they were pure Libby glass! Anyway, on each trip I filled her handbag with Ivory Soap, selling at $50,000 a cake on the streets; so her trips were not in vain. About the time I needed to decide once for all, our host got his permission to advertise. His results were more gratifying to the foreign office than mine had been. A delegation came flocking down from a country hospital which had been independent for years, demanding back wages in fabulous amounts. The foreign office refused to touch the quarrel, just said that no permits would be forthcoming until the issue was settled satisfactorily. So George was absolutely hamstrung. He eventually agreed to pay seventeen million, which was U.S. $850 at current exchange. When he approached me, he still needed ten million, which was exactly what I was trying to dispose of. A few weeks later we met in Hong Kong and he paid me in U.S. funds. Certainly less bother than diamond earrings, and a lot more appropriate for the simple exit I was making!

We busied ourselves at traveling preparations, without much idea of when we might use them. George found a good-sized basket and Esther contributed a blue dress to line it which just matched Julia's eyes. Nell found some curtains that made a pretty ruffled edge, and I fixed a drawstring mosquito net. Julia was used to luxury in the diaper line. Among her first were those made from a new linen tablecloth in Luella's trunk. So I'm sure she was not even impressed at the double-strength outing disposables we made from warm cotton blankets. I prepared a stack of them as high as her basket could hold. When we left she was riding high, but by the time we got to Hong Kong she had hit bottom! I found a letter there from my sister telling me various convenient things for new babies. "I don't suppose you know about disposable diapers," she wrote. "Know about them," I exploded, "I thought I invented them!" They aren't very practical in China, though, for cloth is precious and every time I left one in a cuspidor or any available receptacle, a friendly Chinese would come running after me, wildly waving this pink plaid square, and shouting that I'd forgotten my *pa-dz*.

One of my fellow inmates and good friends was a middle-aged man, alone in China, with little baggage and equally little physical stamina. We had often talked about how fine it would be if we could travel together. About the first of September a slip of paper came, listing only our two names, and saying we were cleared and could go. We were both extremely happy at this provision. Then we unenthusiastically began inquiries into the boat situation. I shrank from three or four days and nights, possibly on the open deck, with a baby not two months old, in the intense heat. The food situation was bad any time, with a bucket plunked down among every six people and everyone reaching in, but with the extreme temperatures upsets were almost a certainty, yet one must eat. Will was not too well, and the trip would have been hard for him. Almost in fun he said, "Wouldn't it be great if there were a plane!" He didn't even have fare, but I was still a millionaire then; so I replied, "I'd pay your way, if you'd see me through the inspections." Still almost joking he called the air office, and to our amazement (oh, we of little faith!) heard that for the first time in weeks there was a plane for civilians, leaving tomorrow, with room for two! "Have your baggage here in two hours."

Next morning we were waving good-by to our Chungking family, and glad as we were to go we really hated to leave them. It had been a rich fellowship, and good growing days. At the air office I found Julia's sweet little basket lining completely torn out. Routine inspections hunt for hidden money, gems, or dope, and I should have thought of that. But the basket served its purpose. After an unbelievably bumpy ride of more than two hours—Julia couldn't even suck her thumb!—

we arrived at Nine Dragon Hills airport. A smiling coolie ignored my gasp as he set Julia, basket and all, upon his shoulder and tossed her into the plane. In three cool hours, instead of four hot days and nights, we were in Hankow. Everybody always has to spend a night there, but our officials were busy and didn't take time for such thorough inspections as usual, transportation clicked, we ran the last stretch, and found ourselves safely on the last ferry to catch the last evening train.

Two families joined the group there, and we were seventeen, eleven children. Children are heart-warmers and ice-breakers, and even the toughest-looking soldiers loved to come to the windows at stops and talk Chinese with them. Sleeping was a problem which only the doctor in the group had solved. He had been traveling many weeks with four children who never got to work off their energy. It was now routine with him to pass out sleeping pills each night. We had only seats, not berths, and sitting got a little old through two nights and a day. Sleeping was impossible, for at each stop Julia woke and screamed. I had to nurse her often in an effort to help the rest of the car sleep. How I thanked God that I could! Life was pretty informal, to be sure, but two English ladies sharing one pair of pajamas tried to keep their standards up. I never could figure out their system. The one with the pajama bottom took off her *blouse* at night, and the one with the top took off her *skirt!* Will and I just sat and drank powdered coffee with powdered milk. On Chinese trains one rents, at the beginning of the trip, a tiny teapot. This is continually being filled from the long-spouted brass teakettle the porter carries, and one has hot water at his finger tips day and night. The wash-hands-water in the rest rooms ran out the first night, and the porter did not approve of our using his boiling water for such unnecessary purposes as washing. But I had a handleless saucepan tucked in Julia's basket, and at night I did cool some water in that to sponge her with. She was black in spite of her net, for the windows were open and the soot was flying.

There was a diner on the train, and Will insisted that I should try to eat something. The five burly Russians on the train happened to be eating there when I arrived. I couldn't read the menu; so I pointed at their fare and said, "I'd like some like that." It looked awfully good—hunks of bread, fried eggs, and slices of some cured meat. But the waiter regretfully told me that was impossible; they had brought it themselves! Others in the group told me later that Russians always carry their own provisions in China. They are technicians for the most part, come to teach the Chinese better ways of doing things. I suppose the idea is that they don't want to be a drain on the country, but I shouldn't be surprised if partly they are afraid to eat what is set before them. Or maybe they just like their own vodka better. I saw too late that I was asking for a bottle of that, too!

We had to stay over a day in Canton, of course, for we got in about the time the morning train for the border left. Here we were subjected to several very thorough searches, including being "felt" over by young girls. Months before, I had seen a German lady standing in the midst of a crowd being forced to pull a property deed out of her foundation garment; so I had no foolish notions about sneaking anything out. There was just one bit of property I cared about, and that was a lively ten pounds of little girl. She was sick by the time we got to Canton, and the doctor had his wife help me give her a crushed sulfa pill. The only way she slept peacefully was riding in a pedicab; so we rode a lot, stout, gray-haired Will and I wedged into one, and Julia taking turns on our knees. We must have made quite a family picture! Some people went shopping to spend their last dollars, but we spent them on rides and hot buttered toast.

Register here, register there, pack, unpack, and pack again, with Will doing the work and I trying to keep him from expressing his opinions. "Just two more days, just one more day, half a day more, another hour, Will," and so he held his tongue and wadded the stuff into the suitcases once more. The train to the border gave us our last dose of propaganda. Trained speakers came through giving lectures to the people about their traveling companions, us. The reason we were going out was that we were of no use in China, and not worth the ammunition to dispose of. Then a pep talk to the Chinese on the train, for they had temporary Hong Kong permits and they might forget their obligations once they got there.

Finally, the last red tape was cleared and we started through. A Chinese girl who had talked her way from Shanghai was sent back at the gate! The last mile consisted of a railroad bridge linking Communist China with the British Colony of Hong Kong. Halfway across the bridge is a barbed-wire barricade with a narrow passage in between. On one side stand Communist soldiers. On the other side are tall, handsome, spotless MP's. The final stare as the guard compares one's picture with the person, the final surrender of that precious scrap of paper, the final walk into freedom—it must take only a few seconds of time, but it seemed a suspense-packed eternity. And the realization that one is there must take a good many months, because I've been out a year, now, and still find it hard to believe.

After a couple of restful weeks in Hong Kong at the MCC Center, Julia and I had both regained our equilibrium and were eager for the last lap. Pan-American Airlines couldn't have been more accommodating, and Julia has never been such a good girl, before or since. We flew on Monday, September 24, in the late afternoon. Forty-eight hours and two Tuesdays later we were thrilling at the lights of San Francisco. Manila was our first stop, where a helpful girl reporter frightened me terribly by disappearing with Julia while I ate. She was walking her in a dark room, but I couldn't find them and thought the baby was kidnapped. Early breakfast at hazy Guam, an afternoon drink of juice at glaring Wake, a very short night as we sped toward the sunrise, and then Honolulu.

A good friend formerly from Chengtu met us there with two gorgeous orchid leis and took us home for a few hours' rest. When we flew again the airline hostess put the orchids in cold storage for our California arrival, but as we approached there and she brought them out, my buxom and inebriated seatmate from Honolulu presented them to two tipsy gentlemen near us. The presentation was prefaced with the traditional *aloha,* and more important to them, the traditional kiss.

I was feeling nearly intoxicated myself, but not from the pink champagne on the captain's dinner menu. After nine long months I was meeting Don, and safely bringing a ten-week-old little daughter to him. She somehow survived our embrace, and though it was past her bedtime she turned on her sweetest smile for her daddy. Doubtless that's where she started her ridiculous habit of laughing in the wee hours of the night. We smiled too, through tears.

L'envoi

Ah, China, our China, with your challenge and your charm, we truly didn't want to leave you. We wanted all of your people to share the good news we had come to tell. Not our news, but meant for the whole world.

Your questing millions need the peace of Him who is our Peace. They need the love of Him who so loved the world that He gave His Son to redeem it. They sorely need the strength and courage which comes to those who hear Him say, "I have overcome the world," and "I am with you always." And they are entitled to a full share of the sure hope of eternal life promised to "whosoever believes in Him."

Though we are miles from you and man-made barriers daily endeavor to separate us still more, yet you are and always shall be in our hearts and prayers. Indeed, a bit of our hearts will always remain in your keeping.

God bless you, dear China, and God help you.